The Pampered Chef®

It's good for you

healthy recipes for busy families

Can great taste and healthier eating go hand-in-hand? With The Pampered Chef's *It's Good for You* cookbook, you'll say "yes!" From appetizers to desserts, you'll find over 60 delicious recipes packed with flavor and geared for today's busy families. You'll love our light, sensible and balanced approach to meal preparation through the creative use of fresh, wholesome ingredients, healthier convenience foods and a variety of cooking techniques. In addition, we've provided helpful nutrition information, tips and ideas to help you lighten up all your family favorites. So, the next time you gather at the table, you can say with confidence, *"It's good for you!"*

Enjoy!

The Pampered Chef Test Kitchens

On the cover: *Spicy Sausage & Peppers Penne* (p. 95)

contents

Gather around the table to enjoy
this collection of updated mealtime
classics and fresh new entrées.

Try our tempting array of dessert treats
that will satisfy even the most discerning
sweet tooth and bring smiles all around.

Guide to Good Nutrition

With nutrition information changing as rapidly as fashion trends, it's easy to become confused about what to eat. However, eating well is easier than you may think, and it *can* include your favorite foods. When all is said and done, health experts agree that the key to healthy, pleasurable eating is the time-tested advice of balanced nutrition, variety and moderation.

Secrets of the Pyramid

The Food Guide Pyramid, which was developed by the U.S. Department of Agriculture and illustrates the seven Dietary Guidelines for Americans, is a practical guide to help you make healthy food choices. The guidelines recommend that you:

- Eat a variety of foods

- Balance the food you eat with physical activity. Maintain or improve your weight

- Choose a diet with plenty of grain products, vegetables and fruits

- Choose a diet low in fat, saturated fat and cholesterol

- Choose a diet moderate in sugar

- Choose a diet moderate in salt and sodium

- If you drink alcoholic beverages, do so in moderation

Using the Food Guide Pyramid allows you to eat a variety of foods so that you can get the nutrients you need daily. The foundation of your diet should include 6-11 servings of bread, cereal, rice and pasta that are high in fiber and complex carbohydrates. Next, 5-6 servings should come from a variety of high-fiber fruits and vegetables. Add 2-3 servings from the dairy group including milk, yogurt and cheese and 2-3 servings from the meat group containing meat, poultry, fish, dry beans, eggs and nuts. Go easy on fats, oils and sweets, which top the pyramid.

Portion Power

To make the most of the pyramid, you need to know what counts as a serving. Following are examples of serving sizes and some common equivalent-sized objects to help remind you of portion size.

	PORTION	OBJECT OF SIMILAR SIZE
BREADS, CEREALS, RICE AND PASTA	1 bagel	Hockey puck
	1 pancake	Compact disc
	1 ounce cereal or ½ cup cooked rice, cereal or pasta	Paper cupcake liner
VEGETABLES	½ cup chopped vegetables, cooked or raw	Fist
	1 cup of raw, leafy vegetables	Palm of hand
	1 potato	Computer mouse
FRUITS	1 medium apple, banana or orange	Baseball
	½ cup chopped, cooked or canned fruit	Tennis ball
	¾ cup fruit juice	Juice box
	¼ cup dried fruit	Handful
MILK, YOGURT AND CHEESE	1 cup milk	
	1 cup yogurt	
	1 ounce cheese	Domino
MEATS, DRY BEANS, EGGS AND NUTS	2-3 ounces lean meat, poultry or fish	Deck of cards
	½ cup cooked dry beans	Tennis ball
	1 large egg	
	2 tablespoons peanut butter	Thumb (joint to tip)

Percent Daily Values

Also known as reference values, following are recommended guidelines based on the assumption that the average adult between the ages of 25 and 50 takes in about 2000 calories a day. Remember, your specific daily values can and do vary depending on your lifestyle, age and circumstances. For example, men need more protein and calories, as do pregnant or breast-feeding women.

▸ **Total fat** – 65 grams or less (or less than 30% of total calories)

▸ **Saturated fat** – 20 grams or less (or less than ⅓ total fat intake)

▸ **Cholesterol** – 300 milligrams or less

▸ **Total carbohydrates** – 300 grams (or 60% of total calories)

▸ **Fiber** – 25-35 grams

▸ **Sodium** – 2,400 milligrams or less

Nutrition Guidelines

All the recipes in *It's Good for You* were developed with 30 percent or less of total calories from fat. Many recipes meet one or more of the criteria for low fat, low cholesterol or low calorie as defined below. It's important to keep in mind that almost all of the recipes can be included in a healthy diet when considered in the context of a daily or weekly meal plan. Since nutrient values are given for each dish separately—and since you'll likely pair an entrée with a vegetable, bread and a side dish of rice, pasta or potatoes—the total percentage of calories from fat for the entire meal will be much lower. We hope that the following guidelines will be helpful in planning both delicious and healthful meals:

LOW FAT	LOW CHOLESTEROL	LOW CALORIE
Main-dish recipes have 10 grams or less fat per serving; appetizers, side dishes and desserts have 3 grams or less fat per serving.	Main-dish recipes have 100 milligrams of cholesterol or less per serving; appetizers, side dishes and desserts have 25 milligrams or less.	Main-dish recipes have 350 calories or less per serving; 400 calories or less per serving for one-dish meals. Appetizers and side dishes have 150 calories or less per serving. Desserts have 250 calories or less per serving.

Fat Facts

It is important to remember that fat is a nutrient that is essential to good health. Fat is a valuable energy source and carries fat-soluble vitamins that are needed to maintain proper growth and development. In addition, fat contributes taste and texture to foods.

Too much fat in the diet can increase your risk of developing heart disease, obesity and other health problems. Health experts agree that fat should not exceed 30 percent of your total daily calories. For example, if you follow a 2,000 calorie diet, then you should consume no more than 600 calories from fat each day. To determine your daily fat intake in grams, simply divide 600 by 9 to reach approximately 65 grams. (One gram of fat equals 9 calories.) *It's important to remember that the 30 percent refers to your total fat intake over time, rather than single foods or meals.* A food high in fat can be part of a healthy diet as long as it's balanced with other lower-fat food choices.

Fats are divided into two types. *Saturated fats*, which are linked to heart disease and raising blood cholesterol, are found in animal foods such as meat, poultry and dairy products. It is recommended that you limit your daily saturated fat intake to 10 percent or less of total calories. *Unsaturated fats* come primarily from plant sources and are linked with reducing blood cholesterol levels.

Simple Substitutions

There are many ways to reduce the amount of unwanted calories and fat in recipes without sacrificing flavor. Following are just a few suggestions for substituting low-fat ingredients for "regular" ingredients in recipes.

INSTEAD OF	SUBSTITUTE
Butter or margarine	Reduced-calorie stick margarine or vegetable oil spread containing at least 70% fat, in baked products
Oil	Nonstick cooking spray for greasing cookware and bakeware Safflower, soybean, canola or peanut oil in reduced amounts; olive or sesame oil for added flavor in recipes
Cheeses: cheddar, mozzarella, Swiss, or cheese blends	Reduced-fat or part-skim cheeses
Cream cheese	Light (Neufchâtel) or fat-free cream cheese in dips and spreads; light or a combination of light and fat-free cream cheese in some baked products
Heavy (whipping) cream	Skim or fat-free evaporated milk
Ice cream	Low-fat or fat-free frozen yogurt or ice milk
Milk (whole)	Reduced-fat or fat-free milk; skim or fat-free evaporated milk
Sour cream	Reduced-fat or fat-free sour cream; low-fat or nonfat yogurt
Whipped cream	Regular, light, or fat-free nondairy frozen whipped topping
Eggs (whole)	2 egg whites or ¼ cup pasteurized egg product for dishes containing eggs; 1 whole egg and 2 egg whites for every 2 whole eggs in baked products
Bacon	Turkey bacon
Ground beef	Extra-lean ground beef; extra lean or lean ground turkey
Luncheon meat	Reduced-fat, fat-free or lean turkey, ham, or roast beef
Poultry	Boneless, skinless chicken breasts or turkey breast slices
Baking chocolate (1 ounce)	3 tablespoons unsweetened cocoa powder and 1 tablespoon (or less) vegetable oil
Nuts	Reduce amount in recipes and toast before adding to recipes

Ingredients for Success

All of the recipes in this cookbook were developed, tasted and tested in The Pampered Chef® Test Kitchens by professional home economists. For optimal flavor and nutritional value, we recommend that you use the ingredients and amounts called for in the recipe. We emphasize fresh ingredients but haven't overlooked the value of high-quality convenience products now available for the way you cook today. You'll find we have successfully used reduced-fat, fat-free, reduced-sodium and "light" products in our recipes without sacrificing flavor. On occasion, you might wish or need to substitute "regular" ingredients for the reduced-fat ingredient listed. These will work equally well; however, the nutritional profile will be affected.

smart
starts

From delicious dips
to fun finger foods,
this offering of light
bites is guaranteed
to get the meal off to
a healthy start.

Coconut Shrimp (p. 10), *Fresh Tomato & Basil Bruschetta* (p. 11), *Savory Canapé French Bread* (p. 11)

Wear plastic gloves when working with jalapeño peppers. The juice from the peppers can create a burning sensation on the skin.

To easily peel and devein the shrimp, insert the split blade of the **Grapefruit Knife** on either side of the shell on the back of the shrimp. With a rocking motion, cut and split the shell up to the tail to easily peel off the shell, leaving tail intact. With pointed end of the split blade, lift out vein. Rinse shrimp under cold running water.

Use the **Egg Separator**, which conveniently attaches to the Small Batter Bowl, to easily separate the whites from the yolks. Eggs separate best when at refrigerated temperature, but egg whites beat to their fullest volume at room temperature. Do not allow any egg yolk to get into the whites or they will not beat properly.

When coating the shrimp with the flaked coconut, it may be necessary to lightly press the coconut onto the shrimp.

Use the **Bamboo Tongs** to easily turn shrimp halfway through baking.

Coconut Shrimp

Behold the sweet taste of the tropics with this shrimp appetizer, which is served with a tangy dipping sauce. (Pictured on p. 8-9)

PREP TIME: 35 MINUTES   BAKE TIME: 16-17 MINUTES

1   lime
2   teaspoons finely chopped fresh jalapeño pepper
½   cup pineapple or peach preserves
1   pound uncooked shell-on large shrimp (about 21-25 count), peeled and deveined
2   egg whites
2   tablespoons cornstarch
1½ cups sweetened flaked coconut

1. Juice lime using **Juicer** to measure 1 tablespoon juice. Remove seeds and finely chop jalapeño pepper using **Food Chopper**. In small **Colander Bowl**, combine lime juice, jalapeño pepper and preserves; mix well. Cover; refrigerate until ready to serve.

2. Preheat oven to 400°F. Line **Rectangle Stone** with **Parchment Paper**. Peel and devein shrimp, leaving tails on. In **Small Batter Bowl**, beat egg whites on high speed of electric mixer until soft peaks form. (Tips of peaks will curl down when beaters are lifted.)

3. Place cornstarch and coconut on two separate plates. Holding shrimp by the tail, coat shrimp with cornstarch. Dip shrimp in egg whites then in coconut to coat. Arrange in a single layer on baking stone. Bake 16-17 minutes or until edges of coconut are deep golden brown, turning once after 8 minutes. Serve with sauce.

Yield: about 2 dozen

Nutrients per serving (3 shrimp, 1 tablespoon sauce):
Calories 240 (25% from fat), Total Fat 7 g, Saturated Fat 4.5 g, Cholesterol 120 mg, Carbohydrate 27 g, Protein 18 g, Sodium 180 mg, Fiber less than 1 g

Diabetic exchanges per serving (3 shrimp, 1 tablespoon sauce):
1 starch, 1 fruit, 2 low-fat meat (2 carb)

Fresh Tomato & Basil Bruschetta

Nothing but the freshest ingredients will do when making this popular appetizer.
(Pictured on p. 8-9)

PREP TIME: 15 MINUTES   BAKE TIME: 10-12 MINUTES

1 loaf *Savory Canapé French Bread* (recipe follows)

3 large ripe tomatoes, seeded and diced (about 1 pound)

½ medium zucchini, coarsely chopped (about ½ cup)

¼ cup snipped fresh basil leaves

1 garlic clove, pressed

2 teaspoons balsamic vinegar

½ teaspoon olive oil

¼ teaspoon salt

⅛ teaspoon ground black pepper

2 tablespoons grated fresh Parmesan cheese

1. Preheat oven to 350°F. Arrange bread slices on flat baking stone. Bake 10-12 minutes or until light golden brown.

2. In **Small Batter Bowl**, combine tomatoes, zucchini, basil, garlic pressed with **Garlic Press**, vinegar, oil, salt and black pepper; mix gently. Using **Medium Scoop**, scoop tomato mixture over bread slices. Sprinkle with Parmesan cheese. Serve immediately.

Yield: 24 appetizers

Nutrients per serving (2 appetizers): Calories 80 (15% from fat), Total Fat 1.5 g, Saturated Fat 0 g, Cholesterol 0 mg, Carbohydrate 14 g, Protein 3 g, Sodium 230 mg, Fiber 0 g

Diabetic exchanges per serving (2 appetizers): 1 starch (1 carb)

30 minutes or less

COOK'S TIPS

Bruschetta is an appetizer typically made with a dense Italian bread, which is toasted and served with fresh toppings.

Store tomatoes at room temperature. Never refrigerate them or they will become mealy and flavorless.

Savory Canapé French Bread

Serve this bread with dips, spreads or soups. (Pictured on p. 8-9)

PREP AND BAKE TIME: 50-60 MINUTES   COOL TIME: 1 HOUR

2 tablespoons (½ ounce) grated fresh Parmesan cheese

2 teaspoons *Pantry Italian Seasoning Mix*

1 package (11 ounces) refrigerated French bread dough

1. Preheat oven to 350°F. Lightly spray inside of **Scalloped Bread Tube** and lids with nonstick cooking spray; place lid on bottom of bread tube. Combine Parmesan cheese and seasoning mix;

sprinkle evenly over bread dough. Fill tube with dough. Place lid on top. Bake, upright, 50-60 minutes. Remove from oven; cool 10 minutes. Remove bread from tube; cool completely. Cut bread into ¼-inch-thick slices.

Yield: 24 slices (1 loaf)

Nutrients per serving (2 slices): Calories 70 (16% from fat), Total Fat 1 g, Saturated Fat .5 g, Cholesterol 0 g, Carbohydrate 11 g, Protein 2 g, Sodium 180 mg, Fiber 0 g

Diabetic exchanges per serving (2 slices): 1 starch (1 carb)

COOK'S TIP

Italian seasoning can be substituted for the Italian Seasoning Mix, if desired.

Margherita Pita Pizzas

Pita bread makes a quick and easy pizza base that's ideal for a variety of speedy toppings. See for yourself!

PREP TIME: 15 MINUTES   BAKE TIME: 10-12 MINUTES

2 teaspoons olive or vegetable oil

1 teaspoon *Pantry Italian Seasoning Mix*

1 teaspoon balsamic vinegar

1 garlic clove, pressed

4 flat pita bread rounds (without pockets)

2 plum tomatoes, sliced

1 cup (4 ounces) shredded part-skim mozzarella cheese

2 tablespoons snipped fresh basil leaves

1. Preheat oven to 425°F. In **Small Batter Bowl**, combine oil, seasoning mix, vinegar and garlic pressed with **Garlic Press**; mix well. Place pita rounds on **Rectangle Stone**. Brush one side of each pita round with oil mixture using **Pastry Brush**.

2. Using **Ultimate Slice & Grate** fitted with v-shaped blade, slice tomatoes. Top pita rounds evenly with tomatoes and cheese. Bake 10-12 minutes or until cheese is melted and edges are lightly browned. Sprinkle with basil. Cut pizzas into quarters using **Pizza Cutter**; serve warm.

Yield: 8 servings

Variation: *Apple & Blue Cheese Pita Pizzas*: Preheat oven to 425°F. In Small Batter Bowl, combine 3 tablespoons blue cheese crumbles and ¼ cup fat-free mayonnaise; mix well. Place pita rounds on baking stone; spread one side of each pita round with 2 tablespoons cheese mixture. Top pita rounds evenly with 1 cored, thinly sliced red apple, 2 tablespoons chopped walnuts and 2 tablespoons additional blue cheese crumbles. Bake as directed above.

Nutrients per serving (Combined average with variation): Calories 135 (27% from fat), Total Fat 4 g, Saturated Fat 1 g, Cholesterol less than 5 mg, Carbohydrate 19 g, Protein 6 g, Sodium 110 mg, Fiber 2 g

Diabetic exchanges per serving (Combined average with variation): 1 fruit, 1 medium-fat meat (1 carb)

LOW CHOLESTEROL

LOW CALORIE

30 minutes or less

COOK'S TIPS

Margherita pizzas are traditionally made with fresh tomatoes, basil and fresh mozzarella cheese, which is packed in whey and has not been aged. Our recipe calls for regular mozzarella cheese, which melts well and is readily available.

For pizzas with tender crusts, choose pita bread rounds without pockets for this recipe.

Ingredients like mozzarella cheese and blue cheese may seem rather indulgent, but when used sparingly, they can fit into a healthy eating plan.

COOK'S TIPS

Medium-grain rice can be found in most grocery stores. The grains are shorter and wider than long-grain rice. When medium-grain rice is cooked, the grains are moist and tender and have a greater tendency to cling together than long-grain rice. Sticky rice, found in Asian food markets, can also be used in this recipe.

Round or square rice wrappers can be found in Asian or specialty food markets.

If desired, 8-inch flour tortillas can be substituted for the rice wrappers—just omit brushing the tortillas with water.

To toast sesame seeds, spread the seeds in a single layer in **Small (8-in.) Sauté Pan**. Toast seeds over medium heat until they begin to brown, stirring frequently. Immediately remove the seeds from the pan and cool completely.

This recipe can be prepared up to 3 hours in advance. Wrap the spring rolls individually in plastic wrap and refrigerate until ready to serve.

Asian Spring Rolls

Serve these pretty appetizers as a first course on stir-fry night.

PREP TIME: 40 MINUTES   COOK TIME: 15 MINUTES   COOL TIME: 20 MINUTES

Dipping Sauce

- 2 teaspoons finely chopped, peeled fresh gingerroot
- 1/4 cup rice vinegar
- 4 teaspoons reduced-sodium soy sauce
- 1 tablespoon sesame oil
- 1 tablespoon sugar
- 1 teaspoon toasted sesame seeds (optional)

Spring Rolls

- 1 cup water
- 1/2 cup uncooked medium-grain rice
- 2 large carrots, peeled and cut into julienne strips
- 1/2 medium cucumber, cut into julienne strips
- 6 (8-inch) rice wrappers
- 3 cups fresh baby spinach leaves
- 12 fresh cilantro sprigs

1. For dipping sauce, finely chop gingerroot using **Food Chopper**. Combine gingerroot, vinegar, soy sauce, oil and sugar in **Small Batter Bowl**; whisk until blended. Sprinkle with sesame seeds, if desired. Cover; refrigerate until ready to serve.

2. For spring rolls, bring water to a boil in **Petite (1½-qt.) Saucepan**. Stir in rice; reduce heat. Cover; simmer 15 minutes. Remove from heat. Cool completely.

3. Cut carrots and cucumber into long julienne strips using **Julienne Peeler**, avoiding cucumber seeds. Moisten both sides of one rice wrapper with water using **Pastry Brush**. Arrange 1/2 cup of the spinach leaves in a single layer on half of wrapper to within 1/2 inch of edges. Top with 1/4 cup rice. Arrange carrots, cucumber and cilantro sprigs evenly over rice. Fold sides of wrapper in toward center; roll up tightly. Repeat with remaining wrappers.

4. Cut each spring roll diagonally into fourths using **Serrated Bread Knife**. Serve with dipping sauce.

Yield: 24 appetizers

Nutrients per serving: Calories 220 (12% from fat), Total Fat 3 g, Saturated Fat 0 g, Cholesterol 0 mg, Carbohydrate 42 g, Protein 6 g, Sodium 210 mg, Fiber 1 g

Diabetic exchanges per serving: 2 starch, 1 fruit (3 carb)

Sweet & Saucy Meatballs

These meatballs are made with lean ground turkey and a tasty fruit glaze. It might be a good idea to double the recipe—these will be sure to disappear!

PREP TIME: 20 MINUTES   BAKE TIME: 30 MINUTES

Meatballs

- ¼ cup chopped onion
- 1 package (1¼ pounds) 93% lean ground turkey
- 1 egg white
- ¼ cup seasoned dry bread crumbs
- 1 teaspoon dried thyme leaves
- 1 garlic clove, pressed
- ½ teaspoon salt

Sauce

- 1 can (8 ounces) jellied cranberry sauce
- ¼ cup ketchup
- ¼ cup orange marmalade
- 2 tablespoons packed brown sugar
- 1 tablespoon Worcestershire sauce

1. Preheat oven to 400°F. Chop onion using **Food Chopper**. In **Classic Batter Bowl**, combine turkey, onion, egg white, bread crumbs, thyme, garlic pressed with **Garlic Press** and salt; mix gently but thoroughly.

2. Using **Small Scoop**, shape meat mixture into balls; place in a single layer over bottom of **Deep Dish Baker**. Bake 15 minutes; drain.

3. Meanwhile, in **Small Batter Bowl**, combine cranberry sauce, ketchup, marmalade, brown sugar and Worcestershire sauce; mix well. Pour sauce over meatballs; mix gently to coat meatballs evenly. Return to oven; continue baking 15 minutes. Stir gently before serving.

Yield: 10 servings (about 40 meatballs)

Nutrients per serving (4 meatballs): Calories 170 (19% from fat), Total Fat 3.5 g, Saturated Fat 1 g, Cholesterol 35 mg, Carbohydrate 23 g, Protein 12 g, Sodium 340 mg, Fiber less than 1 g

Diabetic exchanges per serving (4 meatballs): 1½ starch, 1 low-fat meat (1½ carb)

COOK'S TIPS

To make ahead, prepare meatballs as directed. Bake 25 minutes without sauce. Cool and place in resealable plastic freezer bag for up to 1 month. To reheat, thaw overnight in the refrigerator. Remove from bag and place in baker. Prepare sauce; pour over meatballs and mix gently. Bake at 400°F for 15 minutes or until heated through. Stir gently.

Jellied cranberry sauce is sold in 8- and 16-ounce cans and can be found in the canned goods section of the grocery store. Be sure to buy jellied cranberry sauce, not whole berry cranberry sauce, for this recipe.

This recipe can be easily doubled and prepared in the **Rectangular Baker**.

Mexican Bean Dip

This warm, layered bean dip is a great party appetizer.

PREP TIME: 15 MINUTES   BAKE TIME: 22-25 MINUTES

1 can (16 ounces) 99% fat-free refried black beans

¾ cup (3 ounces) reduced-fat Mexican blend cheese, divided

¾ cup thick and chunky salsa, divided

2 teaspoons lime juice

2 garlic cloves, pressed

2 teaspoons *Pantry Southwestern Seasoning Mix*

¾ cup diced red bell pepper, divided

½ cup whole kernel corn

2 tablespoons snipped fresh cilantro
Reduced-fat sour cream (optional)
Lime Tortilla Chips (recipe follows)

1. Preheat oven to 350°F. In **Classic Batter Bowl**, combine refried beans, ½ cup of the cheese, ¼ cup of the salsa, lime juice, garlic pressed with **Garlic Press** and seasoning mix. Spread bean mixture onto bottom of **Mini-Baker**.

2. Sprinkle ½ cup of the bell pepper and corn evenly over bean mixture. Spoon remaining salsa over corn mixture. Bake 22-25 minutes or until heated through. Top with remaining cheese, remaining bell pepper and cilantro. Garnish with sour cream, if desired. Serve with *Lime Tortilla Chips*.

Yield: 14 servings

Nutrients per serving (¼ cup dip): Calories 60 (27% from fat), Total Fat 2 g, Saturated Fat .5 g, Cholesterol 5 mg, Carbohydrate 8 g, Protein 4 g, Sodium 240 mg, Fiber 2 g

Diabetic exchanges per serving (¼ cup dip): ½ starch, ½ low-fat meat (½ carb)

Lime Tortilla Chips

You'll love these baked tortilla chips with a hint of lime!

PREP TIME: 10 MINUTES   BAKE TIME: 8-10 MINUTES PER BATCH

8 (7-inch) flour tortillas

2 tablespoons lime juice

¼ teaspoon coarse salt

1. Preheat oven to 400°F. Brush one side of each tortilla with lime juice; sprinkle lightly with salt. Cut each tortilla into eight wedges; arrange half of the tortilla wedges in a single layer on **Large Round Stone**. Bake 8-10 minutes or until edges are lightly browned and crisp.

2. Remove from baking stone; cool completely. Repeat with remaining tortilla wedges.

Yield: 64 chips (16 servings)

Nutrients per serving (4 chips): Calories 40 (27% from fat), Total Fat 1.5 g, Saturated Fat 0 g, Cholesterol 0 mg, Carbohydrate 6 g, Protein 1 g, Sodium 170 mg, Fiber less than 1 g

Diabetic exchanges per serving (4 chips): ½ starch (½ carb)

COOK'S TIPS

For a dip with more heat, medium or hot salsa can be used.

Limes and lemons will release the most juice if they are at room temperature. Warm refrigerated limes or lemons in the microwave oven on HIGH for about 10 seconds before juicing with the **Juicer**.

Taco seasoning mix can be substituted for the Southwestern Seasoning Mix, if desired.

30 minutes or less

30

minutes or less

COOK'S TIPS

For added heat, substitute 1 tablespoon seeded and finely chopped jalapeño pepper for the green onions.

Use the **Egg Separator** to easily separate the egg white from the yolk.

Our stainless steel scoops are available in three sizes and are ideal for forming meatballs, making melon balls, scooping cookie dough and portioning batters into pans. The **Small Scoop** yields approximately 1 tablespoon, the Medium Scoop approximately 2 tablespoons and the **Large Scoop** approximately 3 tablespoons.

If desired, the salmon mixture can be formed into larger patties and served as a main dish. Use the Large Scoop to portion the salmon mixture to form 10 salmon cakes (5 servings).

Salmon Cakes with Cool Lime Sauce

A refreshing lime sauce is the perfect complement to these miniature golden salmon cakes.

PREP TIME: 20 MINUTES   COOK TIME: 6-8 MINUTES

Sauce

- 1 lime
- ½ cup fat-free mayonnaise
- ¼ cup fat-free sour cream

Salmon Cakes

- 2 cans (6 ounces each) skinless, boneless pink salmon packed in water, drained and flaked
- ¼ cup finely chopped red bell pepper
- ¼ cup thinly sliced green onions with tops
- 1 tablespoon snipped fresh cilantro
- ¾ cup unseasoned dry bread crumbs, divided
- ⅓ cup fat-free mayonnaise
- 1 egg white

1. For sauce, zest lime using **Lemon Zester/Scorer** to measure 2 teaspoons zest. Juice lime using **Juicer** to measure 2 teaspoons juice. In **Small Batter Bowl**, combine lime zest, juice, mayonnaise and sour cream; mix well. Cover; refrigerate until ready to serve.

2. For salmon cakes, drain salmon using small **Colander**; place in small Colander Bowl and flake using **Pastry Blender**. Finely chop bell pepper and thinly slice green onions using **Chef's Knife**. Snip cilantro using **Kitchen Shears**. Add bell pepper, green onions, cilantro, ½ cup of the bread crumbs, mayonnaise and egg white to salmon; mix well.

3. Sprinkle remaining ¼ cup bread crumbs onto bottom of shallow dish or plate. Using **Medium Scoop**, scoop salmon mixture over bread crumbs; flatten with back of scoop to ½ inch thickness. Turn to coat evenly with bread crumbs.

4. Heat **Family (12-in.) Skillet** over medium heat until hot. Cook salmon cakes 6-8 minutes or until golden brown, carefully turning once with **Nylon Turner**. Serve with sauce.

Yield: 8 servings

Nutrients per serving (2 salmon cakes, 2 teaspoons sauce): Calories 100 (19% from fat), Total Fat 2 g, Saturated Fat 1 g, Cholesterol 15 mg, Carbohydrate 13 g, Protein 8 g, Sodium 290 mg, Fiber less than 1 g

Diabetic exchanges per serving (2 salmon cakes, 2 teaspoons sauce): ½ starch, ½ low-fat meat, 1 vegetable (½ carb)

30 minutes or less

COOK'S TIPS

Hummus is a thick dip of Middle Eastern origin that is made of mashed chickpeas (garbanzo beans), sesame paste, olive oil, lemon juice and garlic.

Our **Simple Additions™ Small Bowl Caddy** will look stylish on any buffet table. It's the perfect carrier for cold dips, spreads and condiments.

30 minutes or less

COOK'S TIP

Crushed dried rosemary can be substituted for the Rosemary Herb Seasoning Mix, if desired.

Quick Hummus Dip

Just a few ingredients are all you need to create this smooth, tangy dip.

PREP TIME: 5 MINUTES

1 container (7-8 ounces) original hummus spread

1 cup (8 ounces) fat-free sour cream

2 teaspoons lemon juice
   Rosemary Pita Chips (recipe follows)

1. Whisk hummus, sour cream and lemon juice in **Small Batter Bowl** using **Stainless Steel Whisk**.

2. To serve, spoon dip into **Simple Additions™ Small Bowl**. Serve with *Rosemary Pita Chips*.

Yield: 1½ cups (12 servings)

Nutrients per serving (2 tablespoons dip, 8 pita chips): Calories 140 (22% from fat), Total Fat 4 g, Saturated Fat .5 g, Cholesterol 0 mg, Carbohydrate 25 g, Protein 6 g, Sodium 370 mg, Fiber 3 g

Diabetic exchanges per serving (2 tablespoons dip, 8 pita chips): 1½ starch, ½ fat (1½ carb)

Rosemary Pita Chips

These savory, crispy chips pair well with hummus or other dips.

PREP TIME: 10 MINUTES   BAKE TIME: 8-10 MINUTES PER BATCH

6 whole wheat pita pocket bread rounds

6 garlic cloves, pressed

1 tablespoon olive oil

4 teaspoons *Pantry Rosemary Herb Seasoning Mix*

1. Preheat oven to 400°F. Split each pita pocket in half horizontally. Using **Garlic Press**, press garlic over rounds; spread evenly. Lightly spray rounds with olive oil using **Kitchen Spritzer**; sprinkle evenly with seasoning mix.

2. Cut each round into eight wedges. Arrange half of the pita wedges in a single layer on **Large Round Stone**. Bake 8-10 minutes or until chips are lightly browned and crisp. Remove from baking stone; cool completely. Repeat with remaining pita wedges.

Yield: 96 pita chips (12 servings)

Nutrients per serving (8 chips): Calories 100 (16% from fat), Total Fat 2 g, Saturated Fat 0 g, Cholesterol 0 mg, Carbohydrate 19 g, Protein 3 g, Sodium 290 mg, Fiber 2 g

Diabetic exchanges per serving (8 chips): 1 starch, ½ fat (1 car

Quick Hummus Dip, Roasted Garlic & Red Pepper Dip (p. 24), Rosemary Pita Chip

COOK'S TIPS

Two heads of garlic may seem overpowering, but once it is roasted, garlic becomes soft and spreadable with a mildly sweet and nutty flavor.

Roasted garlic is delicious spread on slices of warm French bread, tossed with hot cooked pasta or added to mashed potatoes.

Crushed dried rosemary can be substituted for the Rosemary Herb Seasoning Mix, if desired.

This dip can be prepared up to two days in advance. Cover the Small Batter Bowl with the lid and refrigerate until ready to serve.

Roasted Garlic & Red Pepper Dip

The sumptuous flavors of mellow roasted garlic and sweet bell pepper make this dip a sensation worth savoring. (Pictured on p. 23)

PREP TIME: 15 MINUTES   BAKE TIME: 45 MINUTES

2 whole heads garlic, unpeeled
1 large red bell pepper, cut into 1-inch wedges
1 teaspoon olive oil
1 package (8 ounces) fat-free cream cheese, softened
½ cup fat-free sour cream
2 teaspoons lemon juice
½ teaspoon *Pantry Rosemary Herb Seasoning Mix*
   Rosemary Pita Chips (optional, p. 22)

1. Preheat oven to 425°F. Slice about ¼ inch from top of each garlic head to expose garlic cloves. Place in center of **Deep Dish Baker**; surround with bell pepper wedges. Spray garlic and bell pepper with olive oil using **Kitchen Spritzer**; cover with aluminum foil. Bake 40-45 minutes or until garlic is soft; cool completely.

2. Place cream cheese in **Small Batter Bowl**; microwave on HIGH 30 seconds until softened. Whisk vigorously until smooth using **Stainless Steel Whisk**.

3. Remove skin from bell pepper; finely chop using **Food Chopper**. Squeeze garlic cloves from papery skin into batter bowl. Add bell pepper, sour cream, lemon juice and seasoning mix; mix well. Cover; refrigerate at least 1 hour to allow flavors to blend. Serve with *Rosemary Pita Chips*, if desired.

Yield: 1½ cups (12 servings)

Nutrients per serving (2 tablespoons dip): Calories 40 (12% from fat), Total Fat .5 g, Saturated Fat 0 g, Cholesterol 0 mg, Carbohydrates 6 g, Protein 4 g, Sodium 115 mg, Fiber 0 g

Diabetic exchanges per serving (2 tablespoons dip): ½ starch, ½ fat (1 carb)

Deep-Dish Artichoke Focaccia

Preparing this aromatic, savory bread is quick and easy with the help of our Pizza Crust & Roll Mix. (Pictured on p. 34)

PREP TIME: 15 MINUTES   BAKE TIME: 25-30 MINUTES

1 pouch (16 ounces) *Pantry Pizza Crust & Roll Mix* (including yeast packet)

1 tablespoon *Pantry Italian* or *Rosemary Herb Seasoning Mix*, divided

½ cup diced red bell pepper

1 can (14 ounces) artichoke hearts in water, drained and chopped, divided

1¼ cups very warm water (120°F-130°F)

1 tablespoon olive or vegetable oil

2 garlic cloves, pressed

¼ cup (1 ounce) grated fresh Parmesan cheese

1. Preheat oven to 425°F. Lightly spray **Deep Dish Baker** with nonstick cooking spray. In **Classic Batter Bowl**, combine pizza crust mix, yeast packet and 2 teaspoons of the seasoning mix. Dice bell pepper using **Chef's Knife**; set aside. Chop artichokes using **Food Chopper**. Add water and half of the artichokes to pizza crust mix; stir until mixture forms into a ball. Turn dough out onto well-floured surface. With floured hands, gently knead dough 5 minutes. Place dough into baker. Roll dough to edge of baker using lightly floured **Baker's Roller®**.

2. In **Small Batter Bowl**, combine oil, garlic pressed with **Garlic Press** and remaining 1 teaspoon seasoning mix. Brush oil mixture over dough using **Pastry Brush**; top with bell pepper and remaining artichokes, gently pressing vegetables into dough. Grate Parmesan cheese over top using **Deluxe Cheese Grater**.

3. Bake 25-30 minutes or until crust is golden brown. Remove from oven; cool 10 minutes. Remove bread from baker; slice into wedges.

Yield: 16 servings

Nutrients per serving: Calories 120 (15% from fat), Total Fat 2 g, Saturated Fat 0 g, Cholesterol 0 mg, Carbohydrate 23 g, Protein 4 g, Sodium 105 mg, Fiber 2 g

Diabetic exchanges per serving: 1½ starch (1½ carb)

COOK'S TIPS

One 16-ounce package hot roll mix can be substituted for the Pizza Crust & Roll Mix, if desired. You'll find hot roll mix in the baking section of most grocery stores.

Italian seasoning or dried crushed rosemary can be substituted for the Italian or Rosemary Herb Seasoning Mix, if desired.

simple
soups,
salads &
sandwiches

If you're searching
for a quick lunch or
light dinner, you'll
find our selection of
comforting soups,
garden-fresh salads
and satisfying
sandwiches simply
irresistible.

Roasted Tomato & Barley Soup (p. 28), *Portobello Pita Pockets* (p. 29)

Roasted Tomato & Barley Soup

Roasting vegetables draws out natural sugars for flavor while preserving nutrients. In this recipe, the preparation is minimal and the result is a deliciously distinct flavor. (Pictured on p. 26-27)

PREP TIME: 15 MINUTES   COOK TIME: 55 MINUTES

COOK'S TIPS

Lining the pan with Parchment Paper makes cleanup a breeze.

Roasted tomatoes can be served on their own as a healthful side dish or used instead of canned tomatoes in soups and pasta sauces.

Summertime is a great time to take advantage of vine-ripened tomatoes. If tomatoes are not at their peak ripeness, stir 1 tablespoon of sugar into the soup.

Barley is a good source of dietary fiber and it's cholesterol- and sodium-free, low in fat, and a good source of protein, B vitamins and phosphorus. Because it is a significant source of water-soluble fiber, it can help reduce blood cholesterol levels when part of a low-fat diet.

Italian seasoning can be substituted for the Italian Seasoning Mix, if desired.

2 pounds plum tomatoes, cut in half and seeded (about 8-10 tomatoes)

1 tablespoon olive oil

2 tablespoons snipped fresh basil leaves

3 cans (14½ ounces each) 99% fat-free beef broth

1½ cups tomato juice

⅔ cup quick-cooking barley, uncooked

2 garlic cloves, pressed

1 teaspoon *Pantry Italian Seasoning Mix*

½ teaspoon salt

1. Preheat oven to 450°F. Cut tomatoes in half lengthwise; remove seeds using **Cook's Corer®**. Place tomatoes and oil in **Classic Batter Bowl**; toss gently to coat.

2. Line **Stoneware Bar Pan** with 17-inch piece of **Parchment Paper**. Arrange tomatoes, cut side up, in single layer over bottom of pan; bake 45 minutes or until tomatoes start to shrivel. Remove from oven; cool slightly.

3. Remove skins from tomatoes; return tomatoes to batter bowl. Using **Kitchen Shears**, snip tomatoes into small pieces. Snip basil; set aside.

4. In **Professional (4-qt.) Casserole**, combine tomatoes, broth, tomato juice, barley, garlic pressed with **Garlic Press**, seasoning mix and salt. Bring to a boil; reduce heat. Simmer, uncovered, 10 minutes. Remove from heat; stir basil into soup just before serving.

Yield: 6 servings (8 cups)

Nutrients per serving (about 1¼ cups): Calories 160 (17% from fat), Total Fat 3 g, Saturated Fat 0 mg, Cholesterol 0 mg, Carbohydrate 27 g, Protein 9 g, Sodium 540 mg, Fiber 6 g

Diabetic exchanges per serving (about 1¼ cups): 1½ starch, 1 vegetable (1½ carb)

Portobello Pita Pockets

Portobello mushrooms take center stage in these meatless, veggie-packed pita sandwiches. (Pictured on p. 26-27)

PREP TIME: 20 MINUTES   COOK TIME: 8-10 MINUTES

3 tablespoons balsamic vinegar

1 teaspoon olive oil

1 teaspoon *Pantry Rosemary Herb Seasoning Mix*

3 garlic cloves, pressed

¼ teaspoon salt

⅛ teaspoon ground black pepper

1 medium onion, sliced into ½-inch-thick slices

4 medium portobello mushroom caps (3-4 inches in diameter)

2 whole wheat pita pocket bread rounds, cut in half

2 plum tomatoes, sliced

1 cup packed fresh baby spinach leaves

4 slices (1 ounce each) reduced-fat Swiss cheese

1. Combine vinegar, oil, seasoning mix, garlic pressed with **Garlic Press**, salt and black pepper. Set aside 2 tablespoons of the vinegar mixture. Slice onion into ½-inch-thick slices using **Utility Knife**. Using **Pastry Brush**, brush both sides of onion and mushroom caps with remaining vinegar mixture.

2. Heat **Professional Grill Pan** over medium-high heat 5 minutes. Lightly spray pan with oil using **Kitchen Spritzer**. Place pita bread rounds in pan; grill 1-2 minutes on each side. Remove from pan. Place onion and mushrooms in pan; cook 4-6 minutes or until vegetables are tender and have grill marks, turning once.

3. Slice tomatoes using Utility Knife. To assemble sandwiches, cut pita rounds in half. Line each pita round with spinach leaves, one slice cheese, one slice onion, one mushroom cap and tomato slices. Drizzle each pita with reserved vinegar mixture. Serve immediately.

Yield: 4 sandwiches

Nutrients per serving: Calories 220 (28% from fat), Total Fat 7 g, Saturated Fat 3 g, Cholesterol 15 mg, Carbohydrate 29 g, Protein 14 g, Sodium 450 mg, Fiber 4 g

Diabetic exchanges per serving: 1½ starch, 1 vegetable, 1 medium-fat meat (1½ carb)

30
minutes or less

COOK'S TIPS

Store fresh mushrooms in a paper bag in the refrigerator to extend their shelf life. Plastic-wrapped trays and airtight containers trap moisture and can cause mushrooms to spoil quickly. Use mushrooms within 2 days of purchase.

Do not clean mushrooms until you're ready to use them. To remove dirt, wipe mushrooms with a damp paper towel or soft brush, or quickly rinse mushrooms under cold running water and immediately pat dry.

When purchasing pita pocket bread, be sure to buy pita rounds that will form pockets when cut in half.

With 5 grams of fiber per pita bread round, whole wheat pita bread is high in fiber and a good source of complex carbohydrates. Nutrition experts recommend consuming at least 25 grams of fiber each day.

Tropical Turkey and Spinach Salad

Feel the Caribbean breeze as you delve into this vibrant main dish salad, which is served with a tangy dressing.

PREP TIME: 15 MINUTES

30

minutes or less

Dressing

- 3 tablespoons apricot preserves
- 2 tablespoons cider vinegar
- 2 teaspoons olive or vegetable oil
- 2 tablespoons sugar
- 1/4 teaspoon salt
- 1/8 teaspoon ground black pepper

Salad

- 8 ounces 98% fat-free deli roast turkey breast
- 1/2 cup diced red bell pepper
- 1 mango, cut into 1/2-inch cubes (1 cup)
- 2 hard-cooked egg whites, coarsely chopped
- 1/4 small red onion, sliced into thin wedges
- 1 package (6 ounces) fresh baby spinach leaves
- 1/4 cup sliced almonds, toasted

1. For dressing, combine preserves, vinegar, oil, sugar, salt and black pepper in **Small Batter Bowl**; whisk until blended. Cover; refrigerate until ready to use.

2. For salad, slice turkey into 1-inch strips and dice bell pepper using **Chef's Knife**. Cut mango into 1/2-inch cubes using **Utility Knife**. Coarsely chop egg whites using **Food Chopper**. Using **Ultimate Slice & Grate** fitted with v-shaped blade, slice onion into thin wedges.

3. Place spinach in large bowl; add turkey, bell pepper, mango, egg whites and onion. Whisk dressing; pour over salad, gently tossing to coat. Sprinkle with almonds. Serve immediately.

Yield: 4 servings

Nutrients per serving: Calories 240 (30% from fat), Total Fat 8 g, Saturated Fat 1.5 g, Cholesterol 20 mg, Carbohydrate 28 g, Protein 15 g, Sodium 660 mg, Fiber 3 g

Diabetic exchanges per serving: 1 1/2 starch, 1 1/2 medium-fat meat (1 1/2 carb)

COOK'S TIPS

To easily cut a mango, stand it stem end up on **Cutting Board**. Using Utility Knife, cut vertically on flatter side of mango from top to bottom about 1/2 inch to the right of the stem alongside the large, flat seed. Repeat on opposite side. To cut cubes, use tip of knife to score flesh, but not skin, in a crisscross pattern. Bend mango skin back so that the cubes are raised above skin. Run knife under cubes to release the flesh from the skin.

To toast almonds in the microwave oven, place almonds in the **Small Bar Pan**; microwave on HIGH 1-2 minutes or until golden brown, stirring after each 15-second interval. Cool completely.

If desired, 1 cup peach or nectarine slices can be substituted for the mango.

Cheeseburger Hoagie Sandwiches

If you're holding out for a hero, wait no more. Boasting the goodness of lean ground beef, these sandwiches are hearty, tasty and an excellent source of protein.

PREP TIME: 20 MINUTES   BAKE TIME: 26-28 MINUTES

COOK'S TIPS

You are likely to find a wide range of ground beef from ground chuck (20% fat) to ground round (around 11% fat). To reduce the fat of cooked ground beef even more, drain cooked beef in a colander, then press it between layers of paper towels.

Store beef in the coldest part of the refrigerator. Ground beef can be refrigerated from 1 to 2 days, and other cuts of beef can be refrigerated up to 3 days. Ground beef that is wrapped airtight can be frozen up to 3 months; solid cuts for up to 6 months.

For a quick accompaniment, serve this sandwich with carrot sticks and dill pickle spears cut with the **Crinkle Cutter**.

- 1 package (11 ounces) refrigerated French bread dough
- 4 slices (¾ ounce each) American reduced-fat pasteurized process cheese food, divided
- 12 ounces 95% lean ground beef
- ½ cup chopped onion
- 1 garlic clove, pressed
- ¼ cup ketchup
- 2 teaspoons yellow mustard
- 1 cup thinly sliced iceberg lettuce
- 1 plum tomato, sliced

1. Preheat oven to 350°F. Place bread dough on **Cutting Board**; stretch slightly. Cut dough into four equal portions using **Serrated Bread Knife**. Cut three diagonal slits on top of each portion of dough; place seam side down and 3 inches apart, on **Classic Round Stone**. Bake 20-22 minutes or until golden brown. Immediately remove loaves from baking stone to **Stackable Cooling Rack**.

2. Cut two slices of the cheese into small pieces. In **Professional (10-in.) Skillet**, cook and stir beef, onion and garlic pressed with **Garlic Press** over medium heat 8-10 minutes or until no longer pink, breaking beef into crumbles; drain. Stir in ketchup, mustard and cut-up cheese; stir until cheese is melted. Remove skillet from heat.

3. Slice each loaf lengthwise, end to end, cutting halfway through to center of loaf; spread open. Fill evenly with beef mixture; place on baking stone. Bake 6-8 minutes or until bread is toasted and meat mixture is heated through; remove from oven.

4. Cut remaining cheese slices diagonally in half; top each sandwich with one cheese triangle. Top sandwiches with lettuce and tomato slices. Serve immediately.

Yield: 4 sandwiches

Nutrients per serving (1 sandwich): Calories 370 (22% from fat), Total Fat 9 g, Saturated Fat 4 g, Cholesterol 55 mg, Carbohydrate 45 g, Protein 29 g, Sodium 1050 mg, Fiber less than 1 g

Diabetic exchanges per serving (1 sandwich): 3 starch, 2½ low-fat meat (3 carb)

Greek Lemon Chicken Soup

*This soup typically uses eggs to thicken the broth. We've lightened up
the recipe by using fat-free cream of chicken soup.*

PREP TIME: 20 MINUTES   COOK TIME: 17-22 MINUTES

2 cups chopped cooked chicken

2 medium carrots, coarsely
    chopped

1/2 cup chopped onion

1-2 lemons

2 tablespoons snipped fresh parsley

1 garlic clove, pressed

1 can (10 3/4 ounces) 98% fat-free
    reduced-sodium condensed
    cream of chicken soup

3 cans (14 1/2 ounces each)
    100% fat-free chicken broth

1/4 teaspoon ground black pepper

2/3 cup uncooked long-grain
    white rice

1. Chop chicken, carrots and onion using
   Food Chopper. Zest one lemon using
   Lemon Zester/Scorer to measure
   1 teaspoon zest. Finely snip zest using
   Kitchen Shears. Juice lemons using
   Juicer to measure 1/4 cup juice. Snip
   parsley using Kitchen Shears; set aside.

2. Heat **Professional (4-qt.) Casserole** over
   medium heat until hot. Lightly spray with
   nonstick cooking spray. Add carrots,
   onion and garlic pressed with **Garlic
   Press**; cook and stir 2 minutes. Stir in
   chicken, lemon zest, juice, soup, chicken
   broth and black pepper; bring to a boil.
   Stir in rice; reduce heat. Cover; simmer
   over low heat 15-20 minutes or until rice
   is tender. Remove from heat; stir parsley
   into soup just before serving.

Yield: 8 servings (about 10 1/2 cups)

Nutrients per serving (1 1/3 cups): Calories 230 (18% from fat),
Total Fat 4.5 g, Saturated Fat 1.5 g, Cholesterol 45 mg,
Carbohydrate 26 g, Protein 19 g, Sodium 670 mg, Fiber less
than 1 g

Diabetic exchanges per serving (1 1/3 cups): 1 1/2 starch,
1 1/2 low-fat meat, 1 vegetable (1 1/2 carb)

COOK'S TIP

Our cookware is ideal for
those looking to reduce their
fat intake. Its nonstick surface
allows you to cook foods with
a minimal amount of fat,
thereby reducing the total fat
and calories in the recipe. Be
sure to pair our nonstick
cookware with our nylon
tools, which protect the
surface of the cookware.

reek Lemon Chicken Soup, Deep-Dish Artichoke Focaccia (p. 25)

COOK'S TIP

The bread ring can be baked up to 1 day ahead of time. Cool completely, wrap securely in plastic wrap and store at room temperature.

Calypso Club Sandwich Ring

This lively ham sandwich is embellished with pineapple, onion and bell pepper slices.

PREP TIME: 30 MINUTES   BAKE TIME: 26-30 MINUTES

2 packages (11 ounces each) refrigerated French bread dough

1 egg white, lightly beaten

1/2 teaspoon sesame seeds

1/3 cup reduced-fat mayonnaise

1 tablespoon Dijon mustard

2 teaspoons honey

1 medium red bell pepper, thinly sliced

1 medium green bell pepper, thinly sliced

1 small red onion, thinly sliced

2 cups thinly sliced iceberg lettuce

2 cans (8 ounces each) pineapple slices in juice, drained

6 ounces thinly sliced 96% fat-free deli smoked ham

4 ounces thinly sliced reduced-fat Swiss cheese

1. Preheat oven to 350°F. Place bread dough, seam side down, on **Large Round Stone**. Join ends of dough together to form one large ring. Using **Serrated Bread Knife**, make eight diagonal cuts, 1/2 inch deep, on top of dough.

2. Brush egg white over dough using **Pastry Brush**; sprinkle with sesame seeds. Bake 26-30 minutes or until deep golden brown. Immediately remove bread to **Stackable Cooling Rack**; cool completely.

3. Combine mayonnaise, mustard and honey in **Small Batter Bowl**; mix until well blended. Using **Ultimate Slice & Grate** fitted with v-shaped blade, slice bell peppers and onion. Thinly slice lettuce using **Chef's Knife**.

4. To assemble sandwich, cut bread in half horizontally using Serrated Bread Knife. Place bottom half of bread on large serving platter. Spread half of the mayonnaise mixture over cut side of bottom half of bread; top with pineapple slices. Arrange ham and cheese evenly over pineapple; layer with half of the bell pepper slices. Top with lettuce, remaining bell pepper slices and onion slices. Spread remaining mayonnaise mixture over cut side of bread top; place over bottom half. Cut into wedges.

Yield: 8 servings

Nutrients per serving: Calories 340 (25% from fat), Total Fat 9 g, Saturated Fat 3.5 g, Cholesterol 15 mg, Carbohydrate 48 g, Protein 16 g, Sodium 900 mg, Fiber 3 g

Diabetic exchanges per serving: 3 starch, 1 medium-fat meat, 1/2 fat (3 carb)

Mediterranean Tuna Pasta Toss

Solid white albacore tuna is dressed up with fresh vegetables and a lemony vinaigrette for a light and tasty main dish salad.

PREP AND COOK TIME: 30 MINUTES

Vinaigrette

- 1 lemon
- ¼ cup red wine vinegar
- 2 tablespoons olive oil
- 1 teaspoon sugar
- ¼ teaspoon dried oregano leaves
- ¼ teaspoon salt
- ⅛ teaspoon coarsely ground black pepper

Salad

- 2 cups (6 ounces) uncooked medium shell pasta
- 1 small cucumber, scored and sliced (1 cup)
- ½ small red onion, sliced into thin wedges
- 1 cup grape tomatoes, halved
- 10 pitted kalamata olives, coarsely chopped
- 1 package (8 ounces) Mediterranean salad blend (5 cups)
- 1 can (12 ounces) solid white albacore tuna packed in water, drained and flaked
- ½ cup (2 ounces) crumbled feta cheese

1. For vinaigrette, juice lemon using **Juicer** to measure 2 tablespoons juice. Combine lemon juice, vinegar, oil, sugar, oregano, salt and black pepper in **Small Batter Bowl**; whisk until blended and set aside.

2. For salad, cook pasta according to package directions in **Professional (4-qt.) Casserole**; drain and rinse under cold running water.

3. Score cucumber lengthwise using **Lemon Zester/Scorer**. Using **Ultimate Slice & Grate** fitted with v-shaped blade, slice cucumber; cut slices in half. Slice onion into thin wedges. Cut tomatoes in half using **Utility Knife**. Coarsely chop olives using **Food Chopper**.

4. Place pasta in large bowl; add vegetables, olives, salad greens and tuna. Pour vinaigrette over salad, tossing to coat; sprinkle with cheese.

Yield: 6 servings

Nutrients per serving: Calories 280 (30% from fat), Total Fat 10 g, Saturated Fat 2.5 g, Cholesterol 40 mg, Carbohydrate 28 g, Protein 23 g, Sodium 630 mg, Fiber 2 g

Diabetic exchanges per serving: 1½ starch, 2½ low-fat meat, ½ vegetable (1½ carb)

LOW FAT
LOW CHOLESTEROL
LOW CALORIE

30
minutes or less

COOK'S TIPS

The vinaigrette can be prepared ahead of time and refrigerated until ready to use. Mix well before serving.

Kalamata olives are almond-shaped Greek olives with dark purple color and a rich, fruity flavor. They can be found in the deli section or in jars in the condiment section of most supermarkets. Pitted, ripe olives can be substituted for the kalamata olives, if desired.

To reduce both calories and fat, be sure to purchase tuna packed in water for this recipe.

If you're taking this salad to a potluck or picnic, place the salad in the **Chillzanne®️ Bowl**. The bowl has a unique food-safe gel within the bowl's sides that, once frozen, will keep food chilled for hours.

Asian Noodle Bowl

Green onions, fresh gingerroot and Chinese cabbage make this aromatic soup similar to those served in authentic Asian noodle shops.

PREP TIME: 15 MINUTES   COOK TIME: 15 MINUTES

30
minutes or less

- 2 cups diced cooked chicken
- 2 cups thinly sliced bok choy
- ½ cup thinly sliced green onions with tops
- 8 ounces mushrooms, sliced
- ½ cup julienne-cut carrots, 1 inch long
- 1 1-inch piece peeled fresh gingerroot, finely chopped
- 2 garlic cloves, pressed
- 3 cups water
- 1 can (14 ounces) 100% fat-free vegetable broth
- 2 tablespoons reduced-sodium soy sauce
- 1 package (3 ounces) oriental-flavor ramen noodles

1. Dice chicken and thinly slice bok choy and green onions using **Chef's Knife**; set aside. Slice mushrooms using **Egg Slicer Plus®**. Using **Julienne Peeler**, cut carrot into julienne strips; cut strips into 1-inch pieces. Peel gingerroot; finely chop using **Food Chopper**.

2. Place mushrooms, carrots, gingerroot and garlic pressed with **Garlic Press** in **Professional (4-qt.) Casserole**. Add water, broth, soy sauce and seasoning packet from ramen noodles; bring to a boil over medium-high heat. Add chicken, bok choy, onions and noodles. Cover; remove from heat. Let stand 3 minutes. Serve immediately.

Yield: 8 servings

Nutrients per serving (1 cup): Calories 130 (21% from fat), Total Fat 3 g, Saturated Fat .5 g, Cholesterol 30 mg, Carbohydrate 12 g, Protein 13 g, Sodium 580 mg, Fiber 1 g

Diabetic exchanges per serving (1 cup): ½ starch, 1 low-fat meat, 1 vegetable (½ carb)

COOK'S TIPS

Bok choy is a vegetable with tender, dark green leaves and crunchy, white stalks. It is available in supermarkets year-round. Store it, tightly wrapped, in the refrigerator for up to 4 days. Bok choy can be stir-fried with other vegetables; it can also be cooked or served raw on its own. Shredded green cabbage can be substituted for the bok choy, if desired.

Gingerroot has a paper-thin, tan-colored skin that should be removed before use. Store gingerroot in a resealable plastic food storage bag in the refrigerator for up to 3 weeks or in the freezer for up to 6 months. To use frozen gingerroot, just slice off as much as you need.

30

minutes or less

COOK'S TIPS

If desired, 1 container
(6 ounces) frozen avocado
dip, thawed, can be
substituted for the avocado
mixture.

Try dressing up sandwiches
and wraps with a variety of
greens such as peppery
endive, colorful radicchio,
baby spinach leaves or
arugula.

Sprouts, which are
germinated beans and seeds,
are good sources of
phytochemicals (plant
compounds) and antioxidants
that can protect us from
disease. Alfalfa, clover or
spicy radish sprouts are good
choices for this recipe.

Wraps can be prepared in
advance. Wrap filled tortillas
individually in plastic wrap
and refrigerate up to 3 hours
before serving.

California Wraps

*A garden of fresh vegetables, turkey and homemade avocado spread make this
quick sandwich a deliciously healthful choice for lunchtime.*

PREP TIME: 20 MINUTES

- 1 large tomato, seeded and diced
- 6 tablespoons thinly sliced green onions with tops
- 1 medium ripe avocado, seeded
- 1 tablespoon reduced-fat sour cream
- ½ teaspoon lemon juice
- ⅛ teaspoon salt
- 6 (8-inch) fat-free flour tortillas
- 6-12 large lettuce leaves
- 8 ounces thinly sliced reduced-fat deli smoked turkey
- 1 package (4 ounces) salad sprouts (see Cook's Tip)
- 6 tablespoons shredded reduced-fat cheddar cheese

1. Dice tomato and slice green onions using **Chef's Knife.** Using **Avocado Peeler,** cut avocado in half lengthwise; remove seed and cut flesh away from skin. Place avocado in **Classic Batter Bowl;** mash with **Nylon Masher.** Stir in sour cream, lemon juice and salt.

2. Using **Medium Scoop,** top each tortilla with a level scoop of avocado mixture; spread to within ¼ inch of edge using **Small Spreader.** Cover with one or two lettuce leaves, pressing lightly. Place one slice turkey over lettuce. Top evenly with ½ cup salad sprouts; sprinkle with 2 tablespoons tomato and 1 tablespoon each green onion and cheese.

3. Roll up each tortilla tightly. Cut each wrap diagonally in half with **Serrated Bread Knife.**

Yield: 6 sandwiches

Nutrients per serving: Calories 240 (25% from fat),
Total Fat 7 g, Saturated Fat 2.5 g, Cholesterol 20 mg,
Carbohydrate 31 g, Protein 14 g, Sodium 500 mg, Fiber 5 g

Diabetic exchanges per serving: 2 starch, 1 medium-fat meat
(2 carb)

Grilled Vegetable Pasta Salad

Whole wheat pasta and garden-fresh vegetables make this meatless salad a deliciously healthy option for dinner.

PREP TIME: 20 MINUTES   GRILL TIME: 10 MINUTES

7 ounces extra-firm tofu

1 medium red bell pepper, cut lengthwise in half and seeded

1 large yellow squash, cut in half lengthwise

½ pound asparagus spears, trimmed

4 ounces baby portobello mushrooms

½ cup reduced-fat balsamic dressing, divided

¼ cup snipped fresh basil leaves

2 cups uncooked whole wheat rotini pasta

1 ounce (¼ cup) grated fresh Parmesan cheese (optional)

1. Prepare grill for direct cooking over medium coals. Using **Chef's Knife**, slice tofu lengthwise into ½-inch slices. Brush tofu and vegetables with ¼ cup of the dressing using **Pastry Brush**. Snip basil using **Kitchen Shears**; set aside.

2. Meanwhile, cook pasta according to package directions in **Professional (4-qt.) Casserole**; drain and keep warm.

3. Lightly grease grid of grill. Place tofu and vegetables on grid of grill. Grill mushrooms 5-7 minutes and bell pepper, squash, asparagus and tofu 10-12 minutes, turning occasionally with **Barbecue Tongs**. Remove vegetables and tofu from grill.

4. Cut vegetables and tofu into bite-size pieces; place in large **Colander Bowl**. Add pasta, basil and remaining dressing; mix gently. Grate Parmesan cheese over salad using **Deluxe Cheese Grater**; toss gently. Serve warm or at room temperature.

Yield: 4 servings

Nutrients per serving: Calories 290 (28% from fat),
Total Fat 9 g, Saturated Fat 3 g, Cholesterol 5 mg,
Carbohydrate 35 g, Protein 18 g, Sodium 600 mg, Fiber 8 g

Diabetic exchanges per serving: 2 starch, 1 low-fat meat,
1 vegetable, 1 fat (2 carb)

COOK'S TIPS

Tofu, also known as bean curd, is low in fat and high in protein, making it a good substitute for meat in recipes such as salads and stir-frys.

Chinese-style tofu, which is firmer than Japanese tofu, is the best choice for this recipe. It will not fall apart during grilling.

If the tofu you purchased was packaged in water, blot extra moisture from the tofu using paper towels.

To trim asparagus, snap off and discard tough stem ends.

Whole wheat pasta is a good source of dietary fiber. Rotini pasta can be substituted for the whole wheat rotini, if desired.

COOK'S TIPS

This recipe is a great way to use leftover grilled chicken.

The Egg Slicer Plus is a versatile kitchen tool that can be used to slice pitted olives, firm mushrooms and hard-cooked eggs. It works equally well for slicing ripe strawberries, kiwi and bananas.

Chicken Caesar Salad Pizza

Salad gets a delicious makeover! Diced chicken and vegetables are tossed with Caesar salad dressing and served atop a crispy pizza crust.

PREP TIME: 20 MINUTES   BAKE TIME: 12-14 MINUTES

1   **package (10 ounces) refrigerated pizza crust**

3   **cups thinly sliced romaine lettuce**

2   **cups diced cooked chicken**

½   **cup diced red bell pepper**

⅓   **cup pitted ripe olives, drained and sliced**

¼   **cup (1 ounce) grated fresh Parmesan cheese, divided**

½   **cup light creamy Caesar salad dressing**

1   **garlic clove, pressed**

1. Preheat oven to 425°F. Lightly sprinkle **Large Round Stone** with flour using **Flour/Sugar Shaker**. Unroll pizza crust on baking stone, shaping into a circle. Using lightly floured **Baker's Roller**®, roll into a 12-inch circle. Bake 12-14 minutes or until crust is light golden brown.

2. Meanwhile, using **Chef's Knife**, slice lettuce; dice chicken and bell pepper. Slice olives with **Egg Slicer Plus**®. Place lettuce, chicken, bell pepper and olives in large **Colander Bowl**.

3. Grate Parmesan cheese using **Deluxe Cheese Grater**. In **Small Batter Bowl**, combine salad dressing, half of the Parmesan cheese and garlic pressed with **Garlic Press**; mix well.

4. Spread half of the dressing mixture evenly over crust. Add remaining salad dressing mixture to lettuce mixture; toss to coat. Top crust with salad mixture. Sprinkle with remaining Parmesan cheese. Cut into wedges and serve immediately.

Yield: 8 servings

Nutrients per serving: Calories 300 (30% from fat), Total Fat 10 g, Saturated Fat 2 g, Cholesterol 60 mg, Carbohydrate 27 g, Protein 24 g, Sodium 730 mg, Fiber 2 g

Diabetic exchanges per serving: 2 starch, 2½ low-fat meat (2 carb)

Grilled Steak & Potato Salad

Some people are true meat-and-potato lovers at heart, but everyone can feel good about this hearty salad.

PREP TIME: 20 MINUTES GRILL TIME: 13-16 MINUTES

2 garlic cloves, pressed

2 teaspoons dried thyme leaves

1 teaspoon salt

¼ teaspoon coarsely ground black pepper

1¼ pounds boneless beef top sirloin steak, cut ¾ inch thick

3 tablespoons balsamic vinegar

2 tablespoons olive oil, divided

1 tablespoon Dijon mustard

1½ pounds unpeeled potatoes, cut into ½-inch slices

1 medium sweet yellow onion, cut into ½-inch slices

2 medium tomatoes, cut into wedges

6 cups torn romaine lettuce

1. Prepare grill for direct cooking over medium coals. In **Small Batter Bowl**, combine garlic pressed with **Garlic Press**, thyme, salt and black pepper; mix well to form a paste. Spread all but 1 teaspoon of the garlic mixture over both sides of steak. Add vinegar, 1½ tablespoons of the oil and mustard to remaining garlic mixture in batter bowl; whisk until blended and set aside to use as salad dressing.

2. Cut potatoes into ½-inch slices using **Crinkle Cutter**. Slice onion into ½-inch slices using **Utility Knife**. Brush both sides of potato and onion slices with remaining ½ tablespoon of oil.

3. Place steak, potato and onion slices on grid of grill. Grill steak, uncovered, 13-16 minutes for medium rare (145°F) to medium (160°F) doneness and potato and onion slices 10-12 minutes or until tender, turning steak and vegetables occasionally.

4. Remove steak and vegetables to **Cutting Board**. Carve steak crosswise into thin slices. Cut potato and onion slices in half and tomatoes into wedges. Arrange lettuce, steak, potatoes, onion and tomatoes on serving platter; drizzle with reserved dressing. Serve immediately.

Yield: 6 servings

Nutrients per serving: Calories 300 (30% from fat), Total Fat 10 g, Saturated Fat 3 g, Cholesterol 60 mg, Carbohydrate 29 g, Protein 25 g, Sodium 510 mg, Fiber 4 g

Diabetic exchanges per serving: 2 starch, 3 low-fat meat (2 carb)

COOK'S TIPS

Two 10-ounce boneless beef top loin steaks, cut ¾ inch thick, can be substituted for the boneless beef top sirloin steak. Grill, uncovered, 10-12 minutes for medium rare (145°F) to medium (160°F) doneness, turning occasionally.

When purchasing beef, look for brightly colored red or deep red meat. If it is dull or gray, do not purchase it—it is past its peak.

Store beef in the coldest part of the refrigerator up to 3 days.

Either russet or red potatoes work well in this recipe.

Sweet, pale yellow onions such as Maui, Vidalia and Walla Walla are best for grilling. These special varieties are characteristically mild in flavor and exceedingly juicy. Choose onions that are evenly shaped with dry, papery skins. Avoid onions with soft spots. Always store onions in a cool, dry place.

Lean 'N Green Chili

This chili is not only packed with flavor, it is also thick and rich without the addition of cream. The secret? Grated corn tortillas!

PREP TIME: 15 MINUTES   BAKE TIME: 10-12 MINUTES   COOK TIME: 23 MINUTES

8   (6-inch) corn tortillas, divided

2   teaspoons vegetable oil, divided

1   cup chopped poblano chile peppers (1-2 medium) or green bell pepper

½   cup chopped onion

1   pound boneless, skinless chicken breasts, cut into ¾-inch pieces

1   teaspoon ground cumin

1   garlic clove, pressed

2   cans (14½ ounces each) 99% fat-free chicken broth

2   cans (15 ounces each) pinto beans, drained and rinsed

1¼   cups salsa verde (green salsa) or 1 can (10 ounces) green chile enchilada sauce

2   tablespoons snipped fresh cilantro

Preheat oven to 400°F. Cut four of the tortillas in half and stack them one on top of another. Cut tortillas into ½-inch strips using **Chef's Knife**; place in **Classic Batter Bowl** and toss with 1 teaspoon of the oil. Spread in a single layer over bottom of **Stoneware Bar Pan**. Bake 10-12 minutes or until crisp, stirring once. Remove from oven.

2. Meanwhile, remove membranes and seeds from chile peppers; chop with Chef's Knife. Chop onion using **Food Chopper**. Cut chicken into ¾-inch pieces; toss with cumin in **Small Batter Bowl**. Fold one tortilla to fit into **Deluxe Cheese Grater**; coarsely grate into separate small bowl. Repeat for remaining three tortillas; set aside.

3. Heat remaining 1 teaspoon oil in **Professional (4-qt.) Casserole** over medium-high heat. Add chicken; cook and stir 5 minutes. Remove chicken from casserole; add chile peppers, onion and garlic pressed with **Garlic Press**. Cook and stir 3 minutes. Stir in chicken, broth, beans, salsa and grated tortillas. Bring to a boil. Reduce heat; simmer, uncovered, 15 minutes.

4. Snip cilantro using **Kitchen Shears**; stir into chili. Ladle soup into bowls; top with baked tortilla strips.

Yield: 6 servings (about 7½ cups)

Nutrients per serving (about 1¼ cups): Calories 260 (13% from fat), Total Fat 3.5 g, Saturated Fat 0 g, Cholesterol 45 mg, Carbohydrate 32 g, Protein 25 g, Sodium 850 mg, Fiber 5 g

Diabetic exchanges per serving (about 1¼ cups): 2 starch, 2½ low-fat meat, ½ vegetable (2 carb)

COOK'S TIPS

Poblano chile peppers are dark green and are about 2½-3 inches wide and 4-5 inches long, tapering from top to bottom in a triangular shape. They can be found in the produce sections of most supermarkets.

Wear plastic gloves when working with poblano and other varieties of chile peppers. Their seeds and membranes contain oils that can irritate your skin.

Salsa verde, also known as green salsa, is typically made with tomatillos, green chiles and cilantro. It can be found on the grocery store shelf with the other salsas.

If you do not have a Deluxe Cheese Grater, use a food processor with cutting blade to grate the tortillas in Step 2.

30

minutes or less

COOK'S TIPS

Rinsing canned beans before using them reduces the sodium content of the recipe.

Beans are a powerhouse of nutrition. Not only are they high in protein, they are also fat-free and cholesterol-free. Beans are also rich in folic acid, potassium and soluble fiber.

With so many varieties to choose from, adding canned beans to your favorite dishes is quick and easy.

For a quick way to snip fresh cilantro, place the leaves in a small, deep bowl and snip with the **Kitchen Shears**.

Vegetarian Black Bean Burgers

Over the last decade, veggie burgers have become a mainstay on menus. This one outshines restaurant fare and is high in fiber.

PREP TIME: 15 MINUTES   COOK TIME: 6-8 MINUTES

1   can (15 ounces) black beans, drained, rinsed and mashed

¼   cup finely chopped onion

⅓   cup whole kernel corn

¼   cup thick and chunky salsa

1   garlic clove, pressed

2   tablespoons snipped fresh cilantro or parsley

¼   teaspoon salt

⅛   teaspoon ground black pepper

½   cup unseasoned dry bread crumbs

2   egg whites, lightly beaten

4   whole wheat hamburger buns
    Optional toppings: reduced-fat sour cream, salsa and lettuce leaves

1. Mash beans in **Classic Batter Bowl** using **Nylon Masher**. Finely chop onion using **Food Chopper**. Add onion, corn, salsa, garlic pressed with **Garlic Press**, cilantro, salt and black pepper to beans; mix well. Add bread crumbs and egg whites to bean mixture; mix well. Form bean mixture into four round patties, about ½ inch thick.

2. Heat **Family (12-in.) Skillet** over medium heat until hot. Lightly spray pan with nonstick cooking spray; cook patties 6-8 minutes or until lightly browned, turning once with **Nylon Turner**.

3. Place burgers on buns; serve with toppings, if desired.

Yield: 4 sandwiches

Nutrients per serving: Calories 280 (11% from fat), Total Fat 3.5 g, Saturated Fat 0 g, Cholesterol 0 mg, Carbohydrate 49 g, Protein 12 g, Sodium 810 mg, Fiber 6 g

Diabetic exchanges per serving: 3 starch, 1 vegetable (3 carb)

Pronto Pizza Patties

Everybody loves pizza, so incorporating the flavors of pizza into these open-faced sandwiches will surely win raves.

PREP TIME: 15 MINUTES   COOK TIME: 13-16 MINUTES

- 1 pound 93% lean ground turkey
- 1/2 cup seasoned dry bread crumbs
- 1/2 cup diced green bell pepper
- 1/4 cup finely chopped onion
- 1 garlic clove, pressed
- 1 egg white
- 1 can (8 ounces) pizza sauce, divided
- 1/2 cup (4 ounces) shredded reduced-fat mozzarella cheese
- 6 French or Italian bread slices, cut 1/2 inch thick
- 2 teaspoons olive oil
- 1 teaspoon *Pantry Italian Seasoning Mix*

1. In **Classic Batter Bowl**, combine turkey, bread crumbs, bell pepper, onion, garlic pressed with **Garlic Press** and egg white. Add 1/4 cup of the pizza sauce to meat mixture; mix lightly but thoroughly.

2. Form mixture into six oval patties, 1/2 inch thick. Heat **Family (12-in.) Skillet** over medium heat until hot. Cook patties 12-14 minutes or until meat is no longer pink in center, turning once. About 1 minute before patties are done, top with cheese. Remove patties from skillet; keep warm.

3. Wipe skillet clean with paper towel. Brush one side of each bread slice with olive oil; sprinkle with seasoning mix. Heat skillet over medium heat until hot. Place bread slices seasoned side down in skillet. Toast 1-2 minutes or until bread is lightly browned.

4. Place patties on bread slices. Place remaining pizza sauce in **Small Micro-Cooker®**; microwave, covered, on HIGH 45-60 seconds or until heated through. Serve with sandwiches.

Yield: 6 sandwiches

Nutrients per serving: Calories 270 (29% from fat), Total Fat 9 g, Saturated Fat 2.5 g, Cholesterol 45 mg, Carbohydrate 26 g, Protein 22 g, Sodium 510 mg, Fiber 2 g

Diabetic exchanges per serving: 2 starch, 2 1/2 low-fat meat (2 carb)

COOK'S TIPS

Use the **Egg Separator** to easily separate the egg white from the yolk. Refrigerate the leftover yolk and add it to scrambled eggs or French toast batter for tomorrow's breakfast.

Ground turkey should reach a minimal internal temperature of 160°F. Use the **Pocket Thermometer** to determine when the patties are done.

Italian seasoning can be substituted for the Italian Seasoning Mix, if desired.

You can prepare and shape these burgers in advance. Wrap tightly in plastic wrap and refrigerate up to 1 day in advance.

COOK'S TIPS

Leftover cooked chicken can be used to make this pizza in a flash.

Use a barbecue sauce flavored with hickory or mesquite smoke to bring out the biggest barbecue flavor without lighting up your grill.

Our Barbecue Seasoning Mix adds extra smoky flavor to the barbecue sauce.

Barbecue Chicken & Onion Pizza

The addition of turkey bacon and sautéed onion takes this tangy pizza to new heights of flavor.

PREP AND COOK TIME: 20 MINUTES   BAKE TIME: 18-22 MINUTES

1 large onion, sliced

2 plum tomatoes, sliced

4 slices turkey bacon, diced

2 garlic cloves, pressed

½ cup smoky barbecue sauce

2 teaspoons *Pantry Barbecue Seasoning Mix*

2 cups diced cooked chicken

2 packages (10 ounces each) refrigerated pizza crust

1 cup (4 ounces) shredded cheddar & Monterey Jack cheese blend

1 tablespoon snipped fresh parsley

1. Preheat oven to 425°F. Cut onion in half crosswise. Using **Ultimate Slice & Grate** fitted with v-shaped blade, slice onion and tomatoes. Dice bacon using **Chef's Knife**.

2. Heat **Family (12-in.) Skillet** over medium heat until hot. Lightly spray skillet with nonstick cooking spray. Add onion, bacon and garlic pressed with **Garlic Press**. Cook and stir 10-12 minutes or until onion is tender and lightly browned. Stir in barbecue sauce and seasoning mix; remove from heat. Stir in chicken; set aside.

3. Lightly sprinkle **Large Round Stone** with flour. Unroll both packages of pizza dough and arrange side by side on baking stone, shaping into a circle. Using lightly floured **Baker's Roller**®, roll dough to edge of baking stone, pressing seams to seal.

4. Spread chicken mixture over dough to within ½ inch of edge. Arrange tomatoes evenly over top of pizza; sprinkle with cheese. Bake 18-22 minutes or until crust is golden brown. Remove from oven; let stand 10 minutes. Sprinkle with parsley. Cut into wedges.

Yield: 8 servings

Nutrients per serving: Calories 350 (24% from fat), Total Fat 9 g, Saturated Fat 3.5 g, Cholesterol 45 mg, Carbohydrate 46 g, Protein 20 g, Sodium 860 mg, Fiber 2 g

Diabetic exchanges per serving: 3 starch, 2 low-fat meat (3 carb)

Smashed Potato Soup

*This is comfort food at its best! Refrigerated mashed potatoes help
to get a satisfying dinner on the table in no time.*

PREP TIME: 10 MINUTES   COOK TIME: 10 MINUTES

½ cup coarsely chopped carrot

½ cup coarsely chopped celery

1 package (1 pound, 4 ounces)
   refrigerated mashed potatoes

1 can (14½ ounces) 99% fat-free
   chicken broth

½ cup fat-free milk

1 garlic clove, pressed

¼ teaspoon salt

⅛ teaspoon ground black pepper

½ cup reduced-fat sour cream

2 tablespoons snipped fresh parsley

   Optional toppings: sliced green
   onions, reduced-fat shredded
   cheddar cheese and crisply
   cooked, crumbled turkey bacon

1. Coarsely chop carrot and celery using
   Food Chopper. Place mashed potatoes
   in **Medium (3-qt.) Saucepan**. Gradually
   add broth and milk, whisking until mixture
   is smooth using **Nylon Spiral Whisk**. Stir
   in carrot, celery, garlic pressed with
   Garlic Press, salt and black pepper.
   Bring to a boil; reduce heat. Simmer,
   uncovered, 10 minutes.

2. Remove from heat; stir in sour cream and
   parsley. Ladle soup into bowls; top with
   desired toppings.

Yield: 4 servings (about 5 cups)

Nutrients per serving (about 1¼ cups): Calories 180
(29% from fat), Total Fat 6 g, Saturated Fat 2.5 g,
Cholesterol 20 mg, Carbohydrate 27 g, Protein 6 g,
Sodium 850 mg, Fiber 3 g

Diabetic exchanges per serving (about 1¼ cups): 2 starch,
½ fat (2 carb)

LOW FAT

LOW CHOLESTEROL

LOW CALORIE

30
minutes or less

COOK'S TIPS

Refrigerated mashed
potatoes can be found in the
refrigerated dairy case in
most supermarkets. You can
also substitute 3 cups leftover
mashed potatoes for the
refrigerated mashed potatoes.

Mashed potatoes made with
instant mashed potatoes can
be substituted for refrigerated
mashed potatoes. Prepare
6 servings (about 3 cups)
according to package
directions for reduced-fat
mashed potatoes.

Our cookware accessories
such as the **Nylon Masher**
and Nylon Spiral Whisk are
designed to complement our
cookware pieces. They won't
scratch the surface of
nonstick cookware and are
heat-safe up to 428°F.

Cheesy Italian Braid

This delicious braid resembles a calzone, which is a savory turnover made with pizza dough that is rolled, filled and baked.

PREP TIME: 30 MINUTES   BAKE TIME: 20-23 MINUTES

1   pouch (16 ounces) *Pantry Pizza Crust & Roll Mix* (including yeast packet)
1¼ cups very warm water (120°F-130°F)
¼   cup snipped fresh basil leaves, divided
2   plum tomatoes, sliced
2   garlic cloves, pressed
½   cup part-skim ricotta cheese
1   cup (4 ounces) shredded reduced-fat mozzarella cheese, divided
    Salt (optional)
1   egg white, lightly beaten (optional)
2   tablespoons (½ ounce) grated fresh Parmesan cheese

1. Preheat oven to 425°F. In **Classic Batter Bowl**, combine pizza crust mix and yeast packet. Add warm water and stir until mixture forms a ball. Turn dough out onto well-floured surface. With floured hands, knead dough 5 minutes. Sprinkle additional flour over surface as needed to reduce stickiness. Cover; let dough rest 5 minutes.

2. Snip basil with **Kitchen Shears**. Using **Ultimate Slice & Grate** fitted with v-shaped blade, slice tomatoes.

3. Place dough in center of **Rectangle Stone**. Using lightly floured **Baker's Roller®**, roll dough to edges of baking stone. Press garlic over dough with **Garlic Press**; spread evenly using **Small Spreader**. Starting on longest sides of baking stone, cut sides of dough into eight strips, about 1½ inches wide and 3 inches long.

4. Spread ricotta cheese evenly over center of dough. Sprinkle with half of the basil and mozzarella cheese. Arrange tomato slices evenly over filling; season with salt, if desired. Sprinkle with remaining basil and mozzarella cheese.

5. Starting at one end, lift one strip of dough; twist one turn and lay across top of filling. Repeat, alternating strips of dough to form a braid. Fold bottom edges of dough up at ends of braid. Brush with egg white, if desired. Grate Parmesan cheese over braid using **Deluxe Cheese Grater**. Bake 20-23 minutes or until deep golden brown.

Yield: 8 servings

Nutrients per serving: Calories 270 (20% from fat), Total Fat 6 g, Saturated Fat 3 g, Cholesterol 17 mg, Carbohydrate 43 g, Protein 13 g, Sodium 270 mg, Fiber 2 g

Diabetic exchanges per serving: 3 starch, ½ medium-fat meat (3 carb)

COOK'S TIPS

If desired, one 16-ounce package hot roll mix can be substituted for the Pizza Crust & Roll Mix.

Use the **Pocket Thermometer** to accurately check the temperature of the water when making the dough. Water that is too cold will not activate the yeast while water that is too hot will kill the yeast.

Gently wash fresh basil leaves just before using and blot dry with a paper towel. To store, wrap in a damp paper towel, place in a resealable plastic food storage bag and refrigerate up to 1 week.

Brushing the dough with egg white gives it a shiny, golden brown appearance after baking.

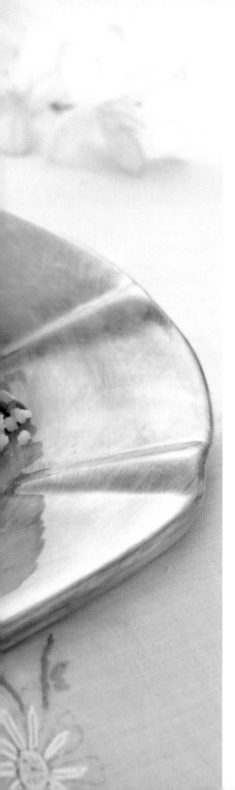

sensational suppers

Bursting with freshness and flavor, our main dish entrées are leaner, lighter and more luscious than ever before. See for yourself!

Caribbean Halibut with Mango Salsa (p. 64), *Quick and Easy Couscous* (p. 65)

COOK'S TIPS

Halibut is a mild, firm-textured low-fat fish that is available in steaks or fillets. Fish steaks are cut crosswise from the fish and are usually ⅝−1 inch thick. Fillets are boneless, lengthwise sections from the sides of the fish.

Fish steaks are best for grilling as they are firm and hold together well during cooking. A general rule for cooking fish is to cook 8-10 minutes per 1 inch of thickness.

Wear plastic gloves when working with jalapeño peppers. The juice from the peppers can create a burning sensation on the skin.

To easily cut a mango, refer to the Cook's Tip on page 31.

If fresh mangoes are not available, use jarred mango slices. They can be found in the refrigerated area of your grocer's produce section. Drain and coarsely chop them for the salsa.

Caribbean Halibut with Mango Salsa

Serve this delicious grilled fish on a bed of couscous with fresh mango salsa.
(Pictured on p. 62-63)

PREP TIME: 25 MINUTES   MARINATE TIME: 30 MINUTES   GRILL TIME: 8-10 MINUTES

Halibut & Marinade

- 4 halibut or swordfish steaks (about 6 ounces each)
- 2 limes
- 1 jalapeño pepper, seeded and finely chopped, divided
- 2 garlic cloves, pressed
- 1 teaspoon olive oil
- ¼ teaspoon salt
- ⅛ teaspoon ground black pepper

Salsa

- 1 mango, coarsely chopped (¾ cup)
- 2 tablespoons finely diced red bell pepper
- 2 tablespoons thinly sliced green onions with tops
   Quick and Easy Couscous (p. 65)

1. For halibut and marinade, rinse halibut and pat dry with paper towels. Zest limes using **Lemon Zester/Scorer** to measure 1 teaspoon zest; set aside for salsa. Juice limes to measure 3 tablespoons juice. Finely chop jalapeño pepper using **Food Chopper**. In **Small Batter Bowl**, combine 2 tablespoons of the lime juice, half of the jalapeño pepper, garlic pressed with **Garlic Press**, oil, salt and black pepper; whisk until blended. Place halibut and marinade in resealable plastic food storage bag; turn to coat. Marinate in refrigerator 30 minutes, turning occasionally.

2. Meanwhile, for salsa, coarsely chop mango using Food Chopper. Finely dice bell pepper and thinly slice green onions using **Chef's Knife**. In **Classic Batter Bowl**, combine mango, bell pepper, green onions, lime zest, remaining 1 tablespoon lime juice and remaining jalapeño pepper; mix gently. Cover; refrigerate until ready to serve.

3. Prepare grill for direct cooking over medium coals. Lightly grease grid of grill. Remove halibut from marinade; discard marinade. Place halibut on grid of grill. Grill, covered, 8-10 minutes or until halibut flakes easily with a fork, turning once using **Barbecue Turner**. Serve with salsa and couscous.

Yield: 4 servings

Nutrients per serving (1 steak, ¼ cup salsa, 1 cup couscous): Calories 390 (13% from fat), Total Fat 5 g, Saturated Fat 1 g, Cholesterol 50 mg, Carbohydrate 42 g, Protein 41 g, Sodium 410 mg, Fiber 3 g

Diabetic exchanges per serving (1 steak, ¼ cup salsa, 1 cup couscous): 2 starch, 1 fruit, 5 low-fat meat (3 carb)

Quick and Easy Couscous

There are plenty of healthy packaged pasta and whole grain side dishes available that will save you time, like this one. (Pictured on p. 62-63)

PREP TIME: 5 MINUTES   STAND TIME: 5 MINUTES

1½ cups 100% fat-free chicken broth
1 cup plain couscous
2 tablespoons snipped fresh cilantro
2 tablespoons sliced green onions
   with tops

1. Bring broth to a boil in **Medium (3-qt.) Saucepan**. Add couscous; stir and cover. Remove from heat; let stand 5 minutes. Add cilantro and green onion; fluff with a fork and serve.

Yield: 4 servings

Nutrients per serving: Calories 170 (2% from fat), Total Fat 0 g, Saturated Fat 0 g, Cholesterol 0 mg, Carbohydrate 34 g, Protein 6 g, Sodium 170 mg, Fiber 2 g

Diabetic exchanges per serving: 2 starch (2 carb)

30
minutes or less

COOK'S TIP

Look for packages of couscous in the rice or pasta section of the supermarket. Couscous is made from durum wheat, the main ingredient in good-quality pastas. This quick-cooking pasta is small and bead shaped. Use plain couscous, not a flavored mix, for this recipe.

Grilled Pita Bread Wedges

This easy side dish goes well with grilled main dishes or cool dips. (Pictured on p. 78)

PREP TIME: 5 MINUTES   GRILL TIME: 3-4 MINUTES

2 whole wheat pita pocket bread
   rounds, cut in half
2 teaspoons olive oil

1. Prepare grill for direct cooking over medium coals. Cut pita bread rounds in half. Brush both sides of each pita half with oil using **Pastry Brush**.

2. Place bread halves on grid of grill. Grill, uncovered, 1½-2 minutes on each side or until lightly browned, turning with **Barbecue Tongs**. Cut bread halves into wedges and serve.

Yield: 4 servings

Nutrients per serving: Calories 110 (25% from fat), Total Fat 3 g, Saturated Fat 0 g, Cholesterol 0 mg, Carbohydrate 18 g, Protein 3 g, Sodium 170 mg, Fiber 2 g

Diabetic exchanges per serving: 1 starch, ½ fat (1 carb)

COOK'S TIP

Whole wheat pita bread is high in fiber (5 grams per bread round) and a wonderful addition to just about any main dish.

Parmesan Chicken and Pasta

Rely on this Italian-inspired chicken recipe for a quick and easy entrée the whole family will love.

PREP TIME: 15 MINUTES   COOK TIME: 20-25 MINUTES

4 frozen boneless, skinless chicken breast halves (3-4 ounces each), thawed

2 egg whites

1 garlic clove, pressed

1 cup fat-free seasoned croutons, grated (½ cup crumbs)

¼ cup (1 ounce) grated fresh Parmesan cheese

1 teaspoon dried oregano leaves

⅛ teaspoon ground black pepper

2 tablespoons all-purpose flour

4 ounces uncooked angel hair pasta

1 jar (14 ounces) tomato and basil spaghetti sauce

¼ cup (1 ounce) shredded reduced-fat mozzarella cheese

1. Preheat oven to 425°F. Using **Kitchen Shears**, remove chicken from package and trim off any visible fat.

2. Using **Mini-Whipper**, beat egg whites in **Classic Batter Bowl** until frothy. Press garlic into egg whites using **Garlic Press**. Using **Deluxe Cheese Grater** fitted with coarse grating drum, grate croutons and Parmesan cheese into shallow bowl. Add oregano and black pepper; mix well.

3. Coat chicken breasts with flour. Dip into egg white mixture. Coat both sides of each chicken breast with crumb mixture, shaking off excess. Discard any remaining crumb mixture. Place chicken on **Classic Round Stone**; lightly spray with nonstick cooking spray. Bake 20-25 minutes or until chicken is no longer pink and juices run clear.

4. Meanwhile, cook pasta according to package directions; drain. Place spaghetti sauce in **Small Micro-Cooker®**. Microwave, covered, on HIGH 2 minutes or until hot. Divide pasta among four serving plates. Top with one chicken breast half, a scant ½ cup spaghetti sauce and 1 tablespoon mozzarella cheese.

Yield: 4 servings

Nutrients per serving: Calories 390 (14% from fat), Total Fat 6 g, Saturated Fat 2.5 g, Cholesterol 75 mg, Carbohydrate 42 g, Protein 40 g, Sodium 780 mg, Fiber 3 g

Diabetic exchanges per serving: 3 starch, 4 low-fat meat (3 carb)

COOK'S TIPS

Using skinless chicken breasts cuts down on added fat while the seasoned coating produces oven-fried flavor and crispness.

Boxes of individually packaged and quick-frozen chicken breasts can be found in the freezer section of most supermarkets and are convenient when you need to get dinner on the table in a flash. To thaw frozen chicken quickly and safely, place in a large bowl in the sink and rinse them under cold running water.

Small boneless, skinless chicken breast halves (3-4 ounces each), found in the refrigerated meat section of the supermarket, can be substituted for the frozen chicken breasts, if desired.

30

minutes or less

COOK'S TIPS

The secret to successful stir-frying is having all the ingredients sliced, chopped and measured before you begin to cook.

For tips on using and storing gingerroot, refer to the Cook's Tip on page 41.

When stir-frying the pork, add the pork to the skillet and let it brown lightly before you begin to stir.

If desired, 1 pound boneless, skinless chicken breasts, cut into thin strips, can be substituted for the pork.

Sesame oil, made from sesame seed, is flavorful oil that is high in polyunsaturated fat. It comes in light and dark varieties, and either is fine to use in this recipe. Look for sesame oil in the Asian food section of your supermarket.

Teriyaki Pork Stir-Fry

Lean pork loin is marinated in Asian seasonings and served with an array of vegetables for an unforgettable dinner.

PREP AND COOK TIME: 30 MINUTES

$2/3$ cup reduced-sodium soy sauce

$1/4$ cup packed brown sugar

1 tablespoon cornstarch

2 teaspoons peeled, finely chopped fresh gingerroot

2 garlic cloves, pressed

$1/4$ teaspoon crushed red pepper flakes

1 pound boneless pork loin chops, cut into $1/8$-inch strips

2 cups uncooked instant whole grain brown rice

1 medium red bell pepper, cut into $1/4$-inch strips

6 ounces fresh snow peas, trimmed

1 bunch green onions with tops, cut into 1-inch pieces (about 6-8)

1 teaspoon sesame oil, divided

1 can (8 ounces) bamboo shoots, drained

1. In **Small Batter Bowl**, combine soy sauce, brown sugar and cornstarch; whisk until blended. Finely chop gingerroot using **Food Chopper**. Add gingerroot, garlic pressed with **Garlic Press** and red pepper flakes to soy sauce mixture.

2. Using **Chef's Knife**, cut pork into $1/8$-inch-thick strips. Add pork to soy sauce mixture; toss to coat. Cover; refrigerate 15 minutes to marinate.

3. Meanwhile, cook rice in **Small (2-qt.) Saucepan** according to package directions. Cut bell pepper into $1/4$-inch strips; trim snow peas and cut green onions into 1-inch pieces using clean Chef's Knife.

4. Heat $1/2$ teaspoon of the oil in **Stir-Fry Skillet** over high heat until hot. Remove pork from marinade using **Nylon Slotted Spoon**; add to skillet, reserving marinade. Using **Bamboo Spatula Set**, stir-fry 1-2 minutes or until pork is no longer pink. Remove from skillet; keep warm.

5. Heat remaining $1/2$ teaspoon oil in same skillet. Add bell pepper, snow peas and green onions. Stir-fry 2-3 minutes or until vegetables are crisp-tender. Return pork to skillet. Stir in reserved marinade and bamboo shoots. Bring to a boil. Cook and stir 1 minute or until sauce is thickened. Serve over rice.

Yield: 6 servings

Nutrients per serving: Calories 310 (19% calories from fat), Total Fat 6 g, Saturated Fat 2 g, Cholesterol 45 mg, Carbohydrate 41 g, Protein 21 g, Sodium 1000 mg, Fiber 4 g

Diabetic exchanges per serving: $2^1/2$ starch, 2 low-fat meat ($2^1/2$ carb)

Italian Market Meat Loaf

Sun-dried tomatoes and zesty Italian Seasoning Mix boost the flavor in a classic Sunday supper.

PREP TIME: 30 MINUTES   BAKE TIME: 1 HOUR, 10 MINUTES   STAND TIME: 10 MINUTES

1	package (3 ounces) sun-dried tomatoes (dry-pack)
2½	pounds 99% lean ground turkey breast
1	cup chopped onion
1	cup fine bread crumbs made from Italian bread (2½ ounces bread)
½	cup (2 ounces) grated fresh Parmesan cheese
¼	cup snipped fresh Italian parsley
1	can (8 ounces) tomato sauce, divided
1	egg
2	garlic cloves, pressed
2	tablespoons *Pantry Italian Seasoning Mix*
1	teaspoon salt
¼	teaspoon ground black pepper
¼	cup red currant jelly, melted

1. Preheat oven to 375°F. Cover sun-dried tomatoes with boiling water; let stand 10 minutes. Drain; coarsely chop using **Chef's Knife**.

2. Place turkey in large **Colander Bowl**. Chop onion using **Food Chopper**. Using **Deluxe Cheese Grater**, grate bread into fine crumbs. Grate Parmesan cheese. Add tomatoes, onion, bread crumbs, Parmesan cheese, parsley, ½ cup of the tomato sauce, egg, garlic pressed with **Garlic Press**, seasoning mix, salt and black pepper to turkey. Mix lightly but thoroughly. Shape meat mixture into loaf in **Stoneware Loaf Pan**. Bake 1 hour.

3. Place jelly in **Small Micro-Cooker**®. Microwave, uncovered, on HIGH 30-45 seconds or until jelly is melted and smooth, stirring after each 15-second interval. Stir in remaining tomato sauce; spoon over meat loaf. Bake an additional 10 minutes or until meat is no longer pink in center of loaf and internal temperature reaches 160°F using **Pocket Thermometer**. Remove meat loaf from pan to serving platter; let stand 10 minutes before slicing.

Yield: 10 servings

Nutrients per serving: Calories 230 (15% from fat), Total Fat 4 g, Saturated Fat 1 g, Cholesterol 70 mg, Carbohydrate 17 g, Protein 33 g, Sodium 750 mg, Fiber 2 g

Diabetic exchanges per serving: 1 starch, 4 low-fat meat (1 carb)

COOK'S TIPS

Sun-dried tomatoes have been dried in the sun creating chewy, intensely flavored tomatoes. They are either dry-packed in bags or packed in oil. Soak dry-packed sun-dried tomatoes in hot water before using. Dry-packed sun-dried tomatoes can be found in the produce or dried fruit section in most supermarkets.

Ground turkey is a good source of low-fat protein. Be sure to choose extra-lean ground turkey breast that is labeled 99% fat free for this recipe.

Italian parsley (also known as flat leaf parsley) is a type of parsley with flat, dark green leaves. It has a stronger flavor than its curly-leaf counterpart. Wash parsley in cold running water, shake off excess moisture and wrap in paper towels. Store in a resealable plastic food storage bag in the refrigerator up to 1 week.

Italian seasoning can be substituted for the Italian Seasoning Mix, if desired.

minutes or less

COOK'S TIPS

The cooking time for fresh pasta is shorter than for dried pasta, so follow the package directions carefully.

Use evaporated milk to add a creamy texture and richness to dishes without adding fat. It is sold in cans and is shelf-stable for up to 6 months, making it a welcome addition to any pantry. Once open, evaporated milk should be stored in the refrigerator and used within 1 week. Be sure not to confuse evaporated milk with canned sweetened condensed milk, which contains sugar and is often used for desserts.

Creamy Spinach Ravioli

Refrigerated cheese-filled ravioli and vegetables are tossed in a velvety sauce for a meatless dish that comes together in no time.

PREP AND COOK TIME: 20 MINUTES

1 package (8 ounces) mushrooms, sliced

½ cup chopped onion

½ cup diced red bell pepper

2 packages (9 ounces each) refrigerated light cheese-filled ravioli

2 garlic cloves, pressed

¼ teaspoon ground black pepper

3 ounces reduced-fat cream cheese (Neufchâtel)

⅓ cup fat-free evaporated milk (see Cook's Tip)

1 package (10 ounces) frozen creamed spinach in low-fat sauce, thawed

Fresh grated Parmesan cheese (optional)

1. Slice mushrooms using **Egg Slicer Plus®**. Chop onion using **Food Chopper**. Dice bell pepper using **Chef's Knife**.

2. Cook ravioli according to package directions in **Professional (4-qt.) Casserole**. Drain and return to casserole; cover and keep warm.

3. Meanwhile, heat **Large (10-in.) Skillet** over medium heat. Lightly spray skillet with nonstick cooking spray; add mushrooms, onion, bell pepper, garlic pressed with **Garlic Press** and black pepper. Cook and stir 3-4 minutes or until vegetables are tender and all liquid is absorbed.

4. Reduce heat to low; add cream cheese and evaporated milk. Stir until cream cheese is melted and sauce is smooth. Stir in creamed spinach. Simmer over low heat 1-2 minutes or until heated through. Pour vegetable mixture over ravioli; stir gently. Serve immediately. Serve with Parmesan cheese, if desired.

Yield: 6 servings

Nutrients per serving: Calories 340 (27% from fat), Total Fat 10 g, Saturated Fat 6 g, Cholesterol 45 mg, Carbohydrate 44 g, Protein 18 g, Sodium 580 mg, Fiber 4 g

Diabetic exchanges per serving: 2½ starch, 1 medium-fat meat, 1 vegetable, 1 fat (2½ carb)

Beef Tamale Bake

In less than an hour, you can serve your family the same great flavors found in traditional tamales.

PREP TIME: 15 MINUTES   COOK TIME: 10 MINUTES   BAKE TIME: 20-23 MINUTES

1½ cups yellow cornmeal

½ cup all-purpose flour

½ teaspoon baking powder

½ teaspoon salt

1 cup hot water

2 egg whites

3 tablespoons 70% vegetable oil spread, melted (see Cook's Tip)

½ pound 95% lean ground beef

1 jar (16 ounces) thick and chunky salsa

1 can (15½ ounces) red beans, drained and rinsed

1 garlic clove, pressed

1½ teaspoons chili powder

½ teaspoon ground cumin

½ cup (2 ounces) shredded Mexican cheese blend

1. Preheat oven to 400°F. Spray **Deep Dish Baker** with nonstick cooking spray. In **Small Batter Bowl**, combine cornmeal, flour, baking powder and salt. Using **Stainless Steel Whisk**, whisk water, egg whites and vegetable oil spread into cornmeal mixture; stir until smooth. Pour batter into baker.

2. Place ground beef in **Large (10-in.) Skillet**. Cook over medium heat 6-8 minutes or until no longer pink, breaking beef into crumbles; drain, if necessary.

3. Add salsa, beans, garlic pressed with **Garlic Press**, chili powder and cumin to beef; mix well. Bring to a boil over medium heat. Spoon beef mixture evenly over batter to within ½ inch of edge of baker. Bake 20-23 minutes or until crust is set. Remove from oven; sprinkle with cheese. Let stand 5 minutes. Cut into wedges.

Yield: 8 servings

Nutrients per serving: Calories 270 (24% from fat), Total Fat 8 g, Saturated Fat 2.5 g, Cholesterol 15 mg, Carbohydrate 39 g, Protein 14 g, Sodium 1050 mg, Fiber 5 g

Diabetic exchanges per serving: 2½ starch, 1 medium-fat meat (2½ carb)

COOK'S TIPS

To reduce calories and fat, this recipe calls for reduced-fat vegetable oil spread that comes in wrapped sticks instead of butter or margarine. We recommend a vegetable oil spread with at least 70% fat.

Other types of beans, such as kidney, black or pinto beans, can be substituted for the red beans, if desired.

To lower the sodium content of canned beans, be sure to drain and thoroughly rinse them before adding them to recipes.

If you can only find 1-pound packages of ground beef, cook and drain the entire amount and freeze half for another use. Place the cooked beef in a heavy-duty resealable plastic food storage bag and freeze up to 3 months.

minutes or less

COOK'S TIPS

If desired, 1½ cups fresh broccoli florets can be substituted for the asparagus.

Frozen potatoes thaw quickly in the microwave. Place them in the **Small Micro-Cooker®** and follow the directions on the package for thawing in the microwave.

Pasteurized refrigerated egg product comes in cartons and can usually be found near the eggs in the grocery store. Made of 99% egg whites, it is a cholesterol-free, fat-free and low-calorie product. Use it in place of whole eggs in many of your favorite egg dishes.

Use the **Small Nylon Turner** to cut the frittata into wedges without damaging the pan's nonstick surface.

Fast 'N Fresh Frittata

A frittata is an open-faced, Italian omelet filled with vegetables. Our version boasts the best of the season with asparagus, chives and potatoes.

PREP TIME: 10 MINUTES   COOK TIME: 20 MINUTES

3 tablespoons snipped fresh chives

1 teaspoon olive oil

½ pound fresh asparagus spears, trimmed and cut into 1-inch pieces

3 cups frozen potatoes O'Brien with onions and peppers, thawed

1 garlic clove, pressed

¾ cup (3 ounces) reduced-fat shredded cheddar cheese, divided

½ teaspoon salt

⅛ teaspoon ground black pepper

1 carton (16 ounces) pasteurized refrigerated egg product

2 small plum tomatoes, sliced
   Additional snipped fresh chives (optional)

1. Snip chives with **Kitchen Shears**. Heat oil in **Large (10-in.) Skillet** over medium-high heat until hot. Add asparagus, potatoes and garlic pressed with **Garlic Press**; cook and stir 4 minutes. Reduce heat to low. Sprinkle chives, ½ cup of the cheese, salt and black pepper over potato mixture. Pour egg product over potato mixture. Cover; cook 14-15 minutes or until egg mixture is set in center. Remove from heat.

2. Meanwhile, using **Ultimate Slice & Grate** fitted with v-shaped blade, slice tomatoes. Arrange tomato slices in an overlapping circular pattern over top of frittata. Sprinkle with remaining cheese. Cover; let stand until cheese is melted. Garnish with additional snipped chives, if desired. Cut into wedges.

Yield: 6 servings

Nutrients per serving: Calories 160 (23% from fat), Total Fat 4 g, Saturated Fat 2 g, Cholesterol 10 mg, Carbohydrate 16 g, Protein 13 g, Sodium 480 mg, Fiber 2 g

Diabetic exchanges per serving: 1 starch, 1½ low-fat meat (1 carb)

Grilled Lemon Chicken with Tabbouleh

Tabbouleh is a chilled Middle Eastern dish made of bulghur wheat flavored with fresh parsley, mint and lemon juice. It is naturally high in fiber and has a bright, fresh flavor.

PREP AND COOK TIME: 25 MINUTES   CHILL TIME: 2 HOURS   GRILL TIME: 12-15 MINUTES

Tabbouleh

- 1½ cups water
- 1 tablespoon olive oil
- ½ teaspoon salt
- 1 cup uncooked bulghur wheat
- 1 large tomato, seeded and diced (1 cup)
- ¼ cup sliced green onions with tops
- 1 cup snipped fresh parsley
- 2 tablespoons snipped fresh mint (optional)
- 1-2 lemons

Lemon Chicken

- 4 boneless, skinless chicken breast halves (4 ounces each)
- 1 tablespoon olive oil
- 1 teaspoon lemon pepper seasoning
- *Grilled Pita Bread Wedges* (p. 65, optional)

1. For tabbouleh, in **Small (2-qt.) Saucepan**, bring water, oil and salt to a boil; stir in bulghur. Cover; remove from heat. Let stand 25 minutes or until water is absorbed.

2. Meanwhile, dice tomato and slice green onions using **Chef's Knife**; place in **Classic Batter Bowl**. Using **Kitchen Shears**, snip parsley and mint. Using **Lemon Zester/Scorer**, zest one lemon to measure 1 tablespoon zest. Juice lemons using **Juicer** to measure ¼ cup juice. Add bulghur, parsley, mint, lemon zest and juice to batter bowl. Cover; refrigerate at least 2 hours to allow flavors to blend.

3. For chicken, prepare grill for direct cooking over medium coals. Rinse chicken; pat dry with paper towels. Brush chicken with olive oil using **Pastry Brush**. Sprinkle with lemon pepper seasoning.

4. Place chicken on grid of grill. Grill, uncovered, 12-15 minutes or until chicken is no longer pink in center, turning occasionally using **Barbecue Tongs**. Remove chicken from grill. Serve chicken with tabbouleh and *Grilled Pita Bread Wedges*, if desired.

Yield: 4 servings

Nutrients per serving: Calories 330 (24% from fat), Total Fat 9 g, Saturated Fat 1.5 g, Cholesterol 65 mg, Carbohydrate 32 g, Protein 32 g, Sodium 500 mg, Fiber 8 g

Diabetic exchanges per serving: 2 starch, 3½ low-fat meat (2 carb)

COOK'S TIPS

Bulghur wheat is a form of cracked wheat that has been steamed and dried for faster cooking. It is a good source of fiber, protein and complex carbohydrates. Bulghur wheat can be found in the specialty or organic section of many grocery stores. It can be stirred into pancake or muffin batter to add a rich, nutty flavor. It can also be used in meat loaf, soups, stews and casseroles.

If desired, 2 cups uncooked instant whole grain brown rice and 1¾ cups water can be substituted for the bulghur wheat and water.

The tabbouleh can be prepared up to 1 day in advance. Store, covered, in the refrigerator until ready to serve.

The **Cook's Corer**® is a handy tool that makes quick work of removing stems and seeds from tomatoes. To seed tomatoes, slice them lengthwise in half using a knife and use the Cook's Corer to scoop out seeds.

Blackened Fish Tacos

*Seasoned tilapia is served atop a bed of crispy slaw and wrapped
in tortillas for a light family supper.*

PREP TIME: 20 MINUTES   COOK TIME: 10-13 MINUTES

Slaw

- ¼ cup sliced green onions with tops
- 2 tablespoons snipped fresh cilantro
- 1 tablespoon fresh lime juice
- 1 tablespoon vegetable oil
- 1 garlic clove, pressed
- 1 teaspoon sugar
- ½ teaspoon Cajun or blackened fish seasoning
- 2 cups broccoli slaw mix

Fish

- 1 pound tilapia fish fillets
- 1 tablespoon Cajun or blackened fish seasoning
- 1 avocado, seeded and sliced
- 8 (6-inch) corn tortillas, warmed
- 3 medium radishes
  Additional snipped fresh cilantro (optional)

1. For slaw, in **Small Batter Bowl**, combine green onions, cilantro, lime juice, oil, garlic pressed with **Garlic Press**, sugar and Cajun seasoning; whisk until blended. Add slaw mix; toss to coat. Cover; refrigerate until ready to serve.

2. Heat **Professional Grill Pan** over medium heat 5 minutes. Moisten fish fillets with water and sprinkle with Cajun seasoning. Lightly spray pan with vegetable oil using **Kitchen Spritzer**. Place fillets in pan; cook over medium heat 10-12 minutes or until fish flakes easily with fork, carefully turning once. Remove from heat. Flake fish into bite-size pieces.

3. Using **Avocado Peeler**, cut avocado in half lengthwise; remove seed and cut flesh away from skin. Cut one avocado half into slices. (Reserve remaining half for another use.) To warm tortillas, place in **Large Micro-Cooker®**. Microwave, covered, on HIGH 1 minute. Top tortillas evenly with slaw mixture and fish. Grate radishes evenly over fish using **Deluxe Cheese Grater**. Top with avocado slices and sprinkle with additional cilantro, if desired.

Yield: 4 servings

Nutrients per serving: Calories 300 (26% from fat),
Total Fat 9 g, Saturated Fat 1.5 mg, Cholesterol 55 mg,
Carbohydrate 32 g, Protein 26 g, Sodium 320 mg, Fiber 6 g

Diabetic exchanges per serving: 2 starch, 3 low-fat meat
(2 carb)

COOK'S TIPS

Tilapia is a native fish of Africa, but it is now farm-raised all over the globe. This low-fat fish is available fresh or frozen. Tilapia has a semi-firm texture and light, sweet flavor.

If desired, catfish fillets can be substituted for the tilapia fillets.

Although avocados have a reputation for being high in fat, don't eliminate them from your diet. Sixty percent of the fat in avocados is monounsaturated, which is the same type of heart-healthy fat found in olive and canola oils. In addition, avocados are cholesterol- and sodium-free and are high in beta carotene, fiber, folate (a B vitamin) and potassium.

Avocados have a thick, pebbled skin that changes from green to purplish black as the fruit ripens. Choose avocados that are free of bruises and store them at room temperature until they reach their full flavor and ripeness. Once ripe, they can be stored in the refrigerator.

30

minutes or less

COOK'S TIPS

Piccata refers to an Italian dish, usually made with thin slices of floured veal that are quickly sautéed and served with a sauce made from the pan juices, lemon juice and fresh parsley. Capers are sprinkled on top to finish the dish.

With the growing popularity of turkey, there are many packaged turkey products available in the meat section of the grocery store. This recipe uses uncooked turkey breast slices that are available in packages containing 6-7 slices per package and are labeled as extra lean.

Capers are the dried flower buds of a bush native to the Mediterranean. They vary in size and are commonly pickled and packed in a vinegar brine. Small jars of capers can be found in the condiment section of most supermarkets. Capers are often used to garnish meat and vegetable dishes.

Turkey Piccata

In just minutes, you can serve your family a classic Italian dish made with lean turkey slices and a light, lemony sauce.

PREP AND COOK TIME: 20-25 MINUTES

1-2   lemons
  1   tablespoon snipped fresh parsley
¼   cup all-purpose flour
½   teaspoon salt
¼   teaspoon ground black pepper
  1   package (17.6 ounces) 99% lean turkey breast slices
  1   tablespoon plus 2 teaspoons butter or margarine, divided
½   cup 100% fat-free chicken broth
  1   garlic clove, pressed
  2   tablespoons capers, drained and rinsed

1. Zest one lemon using **Lemon Zester/Scorer** to measure 2 teaspoons zest. Finely snip zest and parsley using **Kitchen Shears**. Juice lemons using **Juicer** to measure ¼ cup juice; set aside In shallow dish, combine flour, salt and black pepper. Coat both sides of each turkey slice with flour mixture, shaking off excess. Discard any remaining flour mixture.

2. Heat **Family (12-in.) Skillet** over medium-high heat until hot. Place 1 tablespoon of the butter in skillet; swirl until melted. Add turkey to skillet; cook 2 minutes on each side or until turkey is no longer pink. Remove turkey from skillet to platter; keep warm.

3. Add broth, lemon juice, zest and garlic pressed with **Garlic Press** to skillet. Heat over medium heat 1-2 minutes or until sauce is slightly thickened. Add remaining butter to skillet; swirl until melted. Sprinkle capers and parsley over turkey. Carefully pour sauce over turkey slices; serve immediately.

Yield: 4 servings

Nutrients per serving: Calories 140 (28% from fat), Total Fat 4.5 g, Saturated Fat 2 g, Cholesterol 40 mg, Carbohydrate 5 g, Protein 20 g, Sodium 400 mg, Fiber 0 g

Diabetic exchanges per serving: 3 low-fat meat, 1 vegetable (0 carb)

Peppered Beef Filets with Caramelized Onion Mashed Potatoes

These tenderloin steaks cook in no time, making this dish ideal for weeknight entertaining.

PREP TIME: 20 MINUTES   COOK TIME: 26-33 MINUTES

Mashed Potatoes

- 1 cup coarsely chopped onion
- 1 teaspoon 70% vegetable oil spread
- 1 teaspoon sugar
- 1 pound unpeeled red or russet potatoes, cut into 1-inch cubes
- ½ cup fat-free evaporated milk
- 2 tablespoons snipped fresh parsley
- ¾ teaspoon prepared horseradish
- ½ teaspoon salt

Beef Filets

- 2 large garlic cloves, pressed
- 4 beef tenderloin steaks, cut 1 inch thick (5 ounces each)
- 1 teaspoon coarsely ground tri-colored peppercorns or black peppercorns
- ¼ teaspoon salt

1. For mashed potatoes, coarsely chop onion using **Food Chopper**. Melt vegetable oil spread in **Large (10-in.) Skillet** over medium-high heat. Add onion and sugar; cook and stir 8-10 minutes or until onion is tender and deep golden brown. Remove from skillet; set aside.

2. Place potatoes and enough water to cover in **Small (2-qt.) Saucepan**. Cover; bring to a boil. Reduce heat; cook 8-10 minutes or until potatoes are tender. Drain potatoes in small **Colander**; return to saucepan. Using **Nylon Masher**, mash until no lumps remain. Add evaporated milk; stir until well blended. Add reserved onion, parsley, horseradish and salt; mix well. Cover; keep warm.

3. Meanwhile, for beef filets, press garlic into small bowl using **Garlic Press**. Spread garlic evenly over both sides of steaks. Sprinkle tri-colored pepper and salt evenly over both sides of steaks.

4. Heat same skillet over medium heat 5 minutes or until hot. Place steaks in skillet. Cook 10-13 minutes for medium rare (145°F) to medium (160°F) doneness, turning occasionally. Serve with mashed potatoes.

Yield: 4 servings

Nutrients per serving: Calories 360 (29% from fat), Total Fat 11 g, Saturated Fat 4 g, Cholesterol 90 mg, Carbohydrate 28 g, Protein 34 g, Sodium 580 mg, Fiber 3 g

Diabetic exchanges per serving: 2 starch, 4 low-fat meat (2 carb)

COOK'S TIPS

Did you know that horseradish is a knobby white root with a pungent, spicy flavor? It is available fresh in the produce section of grocery stores, but many people opt to buy prepared horseradish, which is pre-ground and jarred. This assertive condiment is great for serving with beef or for adding a snappy flavor to shrimp cocktail sauce.

Beef tenderloin steak is also called filet or filet mignon. It is a very tender, boneless steak cut from the whole tenderloin.

For tips on using evaporated milk, refer to the Cook's Tip on page 72.

Our **Steak Knives** are perfect for cutting through steaks and chops with ease. They come in a set of four with a handy self-sharpening case for easy, safe storage.

COOK'S TIPS

Shrimp are high in cholesterol, but they're low in saturated fat and total fat. You can still enjoy this dish as part of a healthy diet. Just balance your total cholesterol intake for the day.

To easily peel and devein the shrimp refer to the Cook's Tip on page 10.

Frozen shrimp can be substituted for the fresh shrimp, if desired. Simply thaw the shrimp and proceed as recipe directs.

Dried linguine noodles are long, narrow and flat, resembling spaghetti. Fettuccine can be substituted for the linguine, if desired.

Shrimp and Linguine

Who said light entrées have to lack flavor? This classy pasta dish will wow family and dinner guests alike.

PREP AND COOK TIME: 30 MINUTES

¾ pound uncooked shell-on medium shrimp (about 20-30), peeled, deveined and tails removed

¾ cup coarsely chopped carrots (2 medium)

2 large plum tomatoes, seeded and diced

¼ cup sliced green onions with tops

⅓ cup (1½ ounces) grated fresh Parmesan cheese

8 ounces uncooked linguine

1 teaspoon olive oil

2 garlic cloves, pressed

¾ cup reduced-fat sour cream

½ cup fat-free evaporated milk

¼ cup snipped fresh basil leaves

½ teaspoon salt

¼ teaspoon coarsely ground black pepper

Additional grated fresh Parmesan cheese (optional)

1. Peel and devein shrimp; remove tails. Coarsely chop carrots using **Food Chopper**. Dice tomatoes and slice green onions using **Chef's Knife**. Grate Parmesan cheese using **Deluxe Cheese Grater**.

2. Cook pasta according to package directions in **Professional (4-qt.) Casserole**; drain. Return pasta to casserole; cover and keep warm.

3. Meanwhile, heat oil in **Large (10-in.) Sauté Pan**. Add shrimp, carrots and garlic pressed with **Garlic Press**. Cook and stir over medium heat 3-4 minutes or just until shrimp turns pink; remove from skillet and keep warm.

4. Gently heat sour cream and evaporated milk in same skillet over low heat whisking with **Nylon Spiral Whisk**. (Do not boil.) Stir in Parmesan cheese. Add shrimp mixture, tomatoes, green onions, basil, salt and black pepper; mix gently. Pour shrimp and vegetable mixture over pasta; toss gently to coat. Serve with additional Parmesan cheese, if desired.

Yield: 4 servings

Nutrients per serving: Calories 300 (23% from fat); Total Fat 8 g, Saturated Fat 3.5 g, Cholesterol 105 mg, Carbohydrate 37 g, Protein 22 g, Sodium 220 mg, Fiber 2 g

Diabetic exchanges per serving: 2 starch, 2 low-fat meat, 1 vegetable (2 carb)

Zesty Beef Pot Roast Dinner

For a spicy twist to the traditional Sunday dinner, salsa, chili powder and cumin are added to a beef roast and simmered slowly for best flavor.

PREP TIME: 20 MINUTES   COOK TIME: 3 HOURS

 1   tablespoon chili powder

 1   teaspoon ground cumin

 1   teaspoon dried oregano leaves

 1   boneless beef eye of round or beef top round roast (3-3¼ pounds)

 2   garlic cloves, pressed

 1   medium onion, sliced

 1   can (14 ounces) 100% fat-free beef broth

 1   cup thick and chunky salsa

4-5 medium unpeeled red potatoes, cut into 1-inch cubes (about 1 pound)

 1   cup baby carrots

 ¼   cup all-purpose flour

 ½   cup cold water

 2   tablespoons snipped fresh parsley

1. Combine chili powder, cumin and oregano; mix well. Press seasonings evenly over surface of beef roast. Heat **Dutch (6-qt.) Oven** over medium heat until hot; lightly spray with nonstick cooking spray. Press garlic into Dutch Oven using **Garlic Press**. Add roast; brown evenly on all sides, turning occasionally.

2. Using **Ultimate Slice & Grate** fitted with v-shaped blade, slice onion. Separate slices and arrange over roast. Pour broth and salsa over roast. Bring to a boil; cover. Reduce heat to low; simmer 2 hours.

3. Meanwhile, cut potatoes into 1-inch cubes using **Utility Knife**. Add potatoes and carrots to Dutch Oven. Cover; simmer over low heat 1 hour or until meat and vegetables are tender. Remove roast and vegetables to serving platter. Carve roast into ¼-inch-thick slices; keep warm.

4. Place flour in **Small Batter Bowl**; add water and whisk until blended and smooth using **Stainless Steel Whisk**. Gradually add flour mixture to broth in Dutch Oven. Bring to a boil over medium heat, stirring constantly. Boil 1 minute or until thickened. Stir in parsley. Serve gravy with meat and vegetables.

Yield: 8 servings

Nutrients per serving: Calories 250 (19% from fat), Total Fat 6 g, Saturated Fat 2.5 g, Cholesterol 75 mg, Carbohydrate 17 g, Protein 39 g, Sodium 370 mg, Fiber 2 g

Diabetic exchanges per serving: 1 starch, 5 low-fat meat (1 carb)

COOK'S TIPS

The beef eye of round roast is considered a lean but less tender cut of beef. It requires a moist heat method of cooking, such as braising, to tenderize the meat.

Choose a prepared salsa with your preferred heat level for this recipe.

Quick Curried Chicken

There is no need to go out for Thai—this main dish has all the same great flavors but with a fraction of the fat and calories. Light coconut milk is the key ingredient.

PREP AND COOK TIME: 25 MINUTES

3 cups hot cooked white rice

1 medium green bell pepper

1 medium red bell pepper

1 pound boneless, skinless chicken breasts, cut into 1-inch pieces

1 tablespoon ground curry powder

2 teaspoons cornstarch

½ teaspoon ground ginger

¼ teaspoon salt

1 garlic clove, pressed

1 can (14 ounces) light coconut milk

1 can (14 ounces) pineapple chunks in juice, drained

2 tablespoons snipped fresh cilantro leaves

Chopped peanuts or toasted coconut (optional)

1. Prepare rice according to package directions; keep warm.

2. Meanwhile, cut bell peppers and chicken into 1-inch pieces using **Chef's Knife**. In **Classic Batter Bowl**, combine curry powder, cornstarch, ginger and salt; mix well. Add chicken; toss to coat evenly.

3. Heat **Family (12-in.) Skillet** over high heat until hot. Lightly spray pan with nonstick cooking spray. Add chicken and garlic pressed with **Garlic Press**. Cook and stir 6-7 minutes or until chicken is no longer pink. Remove from skillet.

4. Reduce heat to medium-high. Add bell peppers; cook and stir 1-2 minutes. Stir in coconut milk, pineapple and chicken; bring to a boil. Reduce heat; simmer over low heat 15 minutes or until sauce thickens. Add cilantro; mix gently. Serve over rice. Sprinkle with peanuts or toasted coconut, if desired.

Yield: 6 servings

Nutrients per serving: Calories 270 (20% from fat), Total Fat 6 g, Saturated Fat 4 g, Cholesterol 45 mg, Carbohydrate 31 g, Protein 21 g, Sodium 170 mg, Fiber 2 g

Diabetic exchanges per serving: 2 starch, 2 low-fat meat (2 carb)

LOW FAT

LOW CHOLESTEROL

LOW CALORIE

30 minutes or less

COOK'S TIPS

Coconut milk is a canned, unsweetened milk product that is frequently used in Thai cooking. It can be found in the Asian section of your grocery store.

Be sure not to confuse coconut milk with cream of coconut, which is sweetened and used for desserts and mixed drinks.

Curry powder is widely used in Thai and Indian cooking. It is a blend of up to 20 spices, herbs and seeds that give it a distinctive flavor and characteristic yellow color.

When preparing recipes that contain vegetables and raw meat, it's easiest and safest to prepare the vegetables first and set them aside before cutting the meat.

Always wash cutting boards, knives and hands thoroughly in hot, soapy water after cutting raw poultry or meat.

30

minutes or less

COOK'S TIPS

A sea scallop is actually a small round muscle about 1½ inches in diameter that is protected by two beautiful fan-shaped shells. Raw scallops should be creamy white or slightly pink in color and have a distinct sweet odor when fresh.

Sea scallops have a small muscle on the side, which should be removed because it can toughen when cooked. Use the **Paring Knife** to detach the muscle if it has not already been removed at the time of purchase.

Be careful not to overcook scallops or they will become tough and chewy. They are deliciously tender when quickly sautéed, grilled or broiled.

Shallots are small onions with thin, brown, papery skin. Thinly sliced green onions can be substituted for the chopped shallots, if desired.

Pan-Seared Scallops and Spinach

A hot skillet makes quick work of cooking scallops with beautifully browned edges for this elegant, restaurant-style entrée.

PREP TIME: 15 MINUTES   COOK TIME: 12-14 MINUTES

1 pound sea scallops (about 20-24)
  Dash of salt
½ cup diced red bell pepper
2 tablespoons finely chopped shallots
1 lemon
1 teaspoon olive oil
1 package (10 ounces) fresh baby spinach leaves
¼ teaspoon salt
  Dash of ground black pepper
1 tablespoon 70% vegetable oil spread

1. Remove muscle from side of each scallop, if necessary. Wash scallops under cold running water; pat dry using paper towel. Lightly season scallops with a dash of salt.

2. Dice bell pepper using **Chef's Knife**. Finely chop shallots using **Food Chopper**. Zest lemon using **Lemon Zester/Scorer** to measure 1 teaspoon zest. Juice lemon using **Juicer** to measure 1 tablespoon juice.

3. Heat **Family (12-in.) Skillet** over high heat 5 minutes. Add olive oil, bell pepper and shallots; cook and stir 1 minute. Add spinach, lemon zest, juice, salt and black pepper to skillet. Cook 2 minutes or until spinach starts to wilt; remove spinach to serving platter using **Nylon Slotted Spoon**. Pour off any remaining liquid from skillet and discard.

4. Return skillet to heat. Heat over high heat 2-3 minutes or until hot. Lightly spray skillet with nonstick cooking spray. Add scallops and cook 2-3 minutes on each side until golden brown, turning once using **Bamboo Tongs**. Add vegetable oil spread to skillet, tossing scallops to coat. Place scallops over spinach. Serve immediately.

Yield: 4 servings

Nutrients per serving: Calories 160 (28% from fat), Total Fat 5 g, Saturated Fat 1 g, Cholesterol 35 mg, Carbohydrate 8 g, Protein 21 g, Sodium 420 mg, Fiber 2 g

Diabetic exchanges per serving: 2½ low-fat meat, 1½ vegetable (0 carb)

Spicy Sausage & Peppers Penne

Penne pasta is tossed with colorful peppers, zesty sausage and a seasoned tomato sauce—now that's Italian!

PREP AND COOK TIME: 30 MINUTES

30

minutes or less

8 ounces uncooked penne pasta

1 pound hot Italian turkey sausage (about 4 links)

1 *each:* medium green, red and yellow bell pepper, cut into ¼-inch strips

½ cup coarsely chopped onion

2 garlic cloves, pressed

1 can (14½ ounces) diced tomatoes in sauce, undrained

1 can (8 ounces) tomato sauce

2 teaspoons *Pantry Italian Seasoning Mix*

¼ cup (1 ounce) grated fresh Parmesan cheese

1. Cook pasta according to package directions in **Professional (4-qt.) Casserole**; drain and keep warm.

2. Meanwhile, cook sausage in **Family (12-in.) Skillet** over medium-high heat 14-16 minutes or until sausage is lightly browned and no longer pink, turning occasionally. Remove sausages from skillet; cut diagonally into 1-inch pieces and set aside. Cut bell peppers into ¼-inch strips using **Chef's Knife**. Coarsely chop onion using **Food Chopper**.

3. In same skillet, cook bell peppers, onion and garlic pressed with **Garlic Press** over medium heat 6-8 minutes or until peppers are crisp-tender, stirring occasionally. Add sausage, tomatoes, tomato sauce and seasoning mix. Cook and stir 1-2 minutes or until heated through.

4. Place pasta in large bowl; pour sauce mixture over pasta, tossing to coat. Sprinkle with Parmesan cheese. Serve immediately.

Yield: 6 servings

Nutrients per serving: Calories 330 (27% from fat), Total Fat 10 g, Saturated Fat 3.5 g, Cholesterol 50 mg, Carbohydrate 40 g, Protein 21 g, Sodium 980 mg, Fiber 3 g

Diabetic exchanges per serving: 2 starch, 2 medium-fat meat, 1 vegetable (2 carb)

COOK'S TIPS

We've chosen penne for this recipe, which are straight tubes of macaroni that are cut on the diagonal. Other sturdy shapes such as mostaccioli (short tubes), ziti (curved tubes) or rotini (spirals) can be used in this recipe.

Perfectly cooked pasta should be *al dente*—tender but still firm to the bite. Test pasta for doneness before the time stated on the package.

Get a head start on tomorrow's dinner by cooking extra pasta. Drain the pasta thoroughly, then toss it with 1 teaspoon of oil to prevent the pasta from sticking together. Place it in an airtight container or resealable plastic food storage bag and refrigerate up to 3 days. Use it in salads or soups, or toss it with your favorite sauce.

Italian seasoning can be substituted for the Italian Seasoning Mix, if desired.

Glazed Pork Chops with Grilled Apples

Pork chops and apples make a natural pair. Preparing both on the grill gives them a mildly smoky flavor.

PREP TIME: 15 MINUTES   GRILL TIME: 8-10 MINUTES

4 boneless pork top loin or sirloin chops, cut ¾-1 inch thick (about 4 ounces each)

1½ teaspoons *Pantry Rosemary Herb Seasoning Mix*, divided

2 teaspoons finely chopped, peeled fresh gingerroot

⅓ cup apricot preserves

3 tablespoons Dijon mustard

2 medium Braeburn apples, cored and cut crosswise into ½-inch slices

1. Prepare grill for direct cooking over medium coals. Season both sides of pork chops with 1 teaspoon of the seasoning mix.

2. Peel gingerroot; finely chop using **Food Chopper**. Combine gingerroot, preserves, mustard and remaining seasoning mix in **Small Batter Bowl**; mix well. Core apples; cut apples crosswise into ½-inch slices using **Chef's Knife**.

3. Lightly grease grid of grill. Brush one side of apples and pork chops with glaze using **Barbecue Basting Brush**. Place apples and pork chops, glazed side down, on grid of grill. Grill apples 3 minutes and pork 5 minutes, covered, turning once using **Barbecue Turner**. Brush apples and pork chops with remaining glaze. Grill, covered, 3-5 minutes or until internal temperature for pork reaches 160°F for medium doneness.

Yield: 4 servings

Nutrients per serving: Calories 360 (25% from fat), Total Fat 10 g, Saturated Fat 3 g, Cholesterol 95 mg, Carbohydrate 31 g, Protein 38 g, Sodium 500 mg, Fiber 3 g

Diabetic exchanges per serving: 2 starch, 4 low-fat meat (2 carb)

COOK'S TIPS

The pork chops used in this recipe are from the loin section, which is found to be leaner than many cuts of beef and even skinless chicken thighs.

If desired, 1 teaspoon dried rosemary leaves, 1 garlic clove, pressed, ½ teaspoon salt and ¼ teaspoon black pepper can be substituted for the Rosemary Herb Seasoning Mix.

Gala or other red-skinned apples may be substituted for the Braeburn apples.

A quick way to core apples is using **The Corer**™, which removes cores and seeds instantly.

Skinny Chicken Stroganoff

The addition of turkey bacon adds a wonderful,
smoky flavor to an "enlightened" classic.

PREP TIME: 20 MINUTES   COOK TIME: 10 MINUTES

minutes or less

4 slices turkey bacon, cooked and crumbled

6 ounces uncooked extra-broad cholesterol-free egg noodles

¾ cup reduced-fat sour cream

¼ cup all-purpose flour

1 can (14½ ounces) 99% fat-free chicken broth

¼ teaspoon salt

⅛ teaspoon ground black pepper

8 ounces mushrooms, sliced

1 cup chopped onion

1 pound boneless, skinless chicken breasts, cut into ¼-inch strips

1 clove garlic, pressed

2 tablespoons snipped fresh parsley

1. Cook bacon in **Stir-Fry Skillet** over medium heat until crisp. Remove bacon from pan; crumble and set aside.

2. Cook noodles according to package directions in **Professional (4-qt.) Casserole**; drain and keep warm. Meanwhile, in **Small Batter Bowl**, whisk together sour cream and flour until well blended using **Stainless Steel Whisk**. Gradually whisk in chicken broth until mixture is smooth. Stir in salt and black pepper; set aside.

3. Slice mushrooms using **Egg Slicer Plus**®. Chop onion using **Food Chopper**. Slice chicken into ¼-inch strips using **Utility Knife**. Heat skillet over high heat until hot. Add chicken; cook and stir 5 minutes or until no longer pink. Remove from skillet; keep warm.

4. Reduce heat to medium. Add mushrooms, onion and garlic pressed with **Garlic Press**. Cook and stir 3 minutes. Return chicken and reserved bacon to skillet. Stir in sour cream mixture; bring to a boil. Reduce heat and simmer 2 minutes, stirring constantly. Stir in parsley; serve over noodles.

Yield: 6 servings

Nutrients per serving: Calories 300 (22% from fat), Total Fat 7 g, Saturated Fat 3 g, Cholesterol 70 mg, Carbohydrate 31 g, Protein 27 g, Sodium 590 mg, Fiber 3 g

Diabetic exchanges per serving: 2 starch, 3 low-fat meat (2 carb)

COOK'S TIPS

Cholesterol-free egg noodles have the same taste and texture as regular egg noodles. They are made with enriched flour, enriched corn flour and dried egg whites and do not contain egg yolks. They can be found in the dry pasta section of most supermarkets.

To achieve a smooth, velvety sauce, it is important to whisk the sour cream, flour and chicken broth using a wire whisk. The Stainless Steel Whisk does the job beautifully.

You can slice fresh mushrooms in no time using the Egg Slicer Plus. For best results, choose fresh, firm mushrooms. Wipe mushrooms clean with a damp paper towel and trim off stem ends. Place each mushroom stem end up in the egg slicer and slice.

COOK'S TIPS

Cut leftover turkey or chicken into cubes and place in a resealable plastic freezer bag. Label and freeze up to 1 month. Use in all your favorite recipes calling for cooked turkey or chicken.

Eggs will separate more easily when cold. Use the **Egg Separator**, which conveniently attaches to the rim of most bowls, to separate the egg yolk from the egg white.

Reduced-fat all-purpose baking mix is a packaged mix used for making pancakes, biscuits and other baked items. It can be found in the baking section of the grocery near the flour and other packaged baking mixes.

Turkey Vegetable Cobbler

This savory, homestyle dish incorporates fresh vegetables and pre-cooked turkey for a quick and comforting family dinner.

PREP TIME: 15 MINUTES   BAKE TIME: 30-35 MINUTES

Turkey & Vegetable Filling

  2   **cups diced cooked turkey or chicken**
  1   **cup sliced carrots**
  1/2 **cup chopped onion**
  2   **cups broccoli florets**
  1   **can (10¾ ounces) 98% fat-free reduced-sodium condensed cream of chicken soup**
  1/2 **cup 100% fat-free chicken broth**
  1/2 **cup 2% reduced-fat milk**
  1   **garlic clove, pressed**
  1/4 **teaspoon dried thyme leaves**
  1/8 **teaspoon ground black pepper**

Biscuit Topping

  1¼ **cups reduced-fat all-purpose baking mix**
  1/2 **cup 2% reduced-fat milk**
  1   **egg white**

1. Preheat oven to 400°F. For turkey and vegetable filling, cut turkey into ½-inch cubes with **Chef's Knife**. Cut carrots into ¼-inch slices using **Crinkle Cutter**. Chop onion using **Food Chopper**. In **Large Micro-Cooker®**, combine carrots, onion and broccoli. Microwave, covered, on HIGH 2-3 minutes or until crisp-tender; drain.

2. Meanwhile, in **Classic Batter Bowl**, combine soup, broth, milk, garlic pressed with **Garlic Press**, thyme and black pepper; whisk until blended using **Stainless Steel Whisk**. Stir in turkey and vegetable mixture; mix well. Pour into **Deep Dish Baker**.

3. For biscuit topping, in **Small Batter Bowl** combine baking mix, milk and egg white; stir just until dry ingredients are moistened and mixture forms a soft dough. Using **Medium Scoop**, drop six scoops of dough over filling. Bake 30-35 minutes or until topping is golden brown.

Yield: 6 servings

Nutrients per serving: Calories: 270 (21% calories from fat), Total Fat 6 g, Saturated Fat 2 g, Cholesterol 50 mg, Carbohydrate 30 g, Protein 23 g, Sodium 640 mg, Fiber 2 g

Diabetic exchanges per serving: 2 starch, 2 low-fat meat (2 carb)

Oven Barbecue Chili

*This hearty baked chili, loaded with tender beef and
smoky barbecue sauce, conjures images of the Wild West.*

PREP TIME: 40 MINUTES   BAKE TIME: 2 HOURS, 30 MINUTES

2 pounds boneless beef chuck pot
  roast or beef stew meat, cut into
  1/2-inch cubes

4 garlic cloves, pressed

2 cups coarsely chopped onions

2 cups diced green bell pepper

2 cans (15 ounces each) black
  beans, drained and rinsed

2 cans (14.5 ounces each) diced
  tomatoes in sauce, undrained

1 can (8 ounces) tomato sauce

3/4 cup smoky barbecue sauce

2 tablespoons cider vinegar

2 tablespoons chili powder

  Optional toppings: reduced-fat
  shredded cheddar cheese,
  reduced-fat sour cream and
  sliced green onions

1. Preheat oven to 350°F. Trim any visible
   fat from meat using **Chef's Knife**; cut
   meat into 1/2-inch cubes and place in
   Stoneware Baking Bowl. Press garlic
   over meat using **Garlic Press**. Coarsely
   chop onions using **Food Chopper**. Dice
   bell pepper using Chef's Knife. Add
   onions, bell pepper, beans, tomatoes,
   tomato sauce, barbecue sauce, vinegar
   and chili powder to baking bowl;
   mix well.

2. Cover bowl with **Deep Dish Baker**. Bake
   2½ hours or until meat is tender. Using
   Oven Mitts, carefully remove baker from
   baking bowl, lifting away from you. Serve
   with toppings, if desired.

Yield: 12 servings

Nutrients per serving (1 cup): Calories 260 (24% from fat),
Total Fat 7 g, Saturated Fat 2.5 g, Cholesterol 75 mg,
Carbohydrate 20 g, Protein 28 g, Sodium 540 mg, Fiber 4 g

Diabetic exchanges per serving (1 cup): 1 starch, 3 low-fat
meat, 1 vegetable (1 carb)

COOK'S TIPS

Chili is a dish with many
faces that differs widely by
region of the U.S. and by
people's personal palettes. In
Texas, you'll find chili made
of cubed beef, but beans in
Texas chili are often
considered taboo. Cincinnati
chili is made of tomatoes and
ground beef. It is spiced with
cinnamon, cloves and often
chocolate and coffee, and it is
served over cooked spaghetti.

Other varieties of canned
beans such as kidney, Great
Northern or red beans can be
substituted for the black
beans. Be sure to drain and
thoroughly rinse the beans
before adding them to recipes
to reduce their sodium
content.

Choose your favorite prepared
smoky or mesquite barbecue
sauce for this hearty oven
chili.

Rosemary-Crusted Pork Tenderloin with Vegetables

Have the family over for a sensational one-dish meal complete with roasted potatoes and vegetables.

PREP TIME: 20 MINUTES   COOK TIME: 25-30 MINUTES

Pork

- 2 pork tenderloins (about 1 pound each)
- 1 garlic clove, pressed
- 2 tablespoons *Pantry Rosemary Herb Seasoning Mix*
- 1/2 teaspoon salt

Vegetables

- 1 1/2 pounds unpeeled small red potatoes
- 1 large red bell pepper, cut into 1-inch pieces
- 1 medium onion, cut into 1/4-inch-thick wedges
- 1 tablespoon olive oil
- 2 garlic cloves, pressed
- 1 teaspoon Pantry Rosemary Herb Seasoning Mix
- 1/2 teaspoon salt
- 1/4 teaspoon coarsely ground black pepper

1. Preheat oven to 450°F. Place pork tenderloins side by side but not touching in **Stoneware Bar Pan**. Rub surface of pork with garlic pressed with **Garlic Press**. In small bowl, combine seasoning mix and salt. Rub over entire surface of pork.

2. For vegetables, cut potatoes in half or in quarters, depending on size, using **Crinkle Cutter**. Cut bell pepper into 1-inch pieces using **Chef's Knife**. Slice onion into 1/4-inch-thick wedges. In large **Colander Bowl**, combine oil, garlic pressed with Garlic Press, seasoning mix, salt and black pepper; mix well. Add vegetables; toss to coat.

3. Place vegetables in pan surrounding pork. Bake 25-30 minutes or until **Pocket Thermometer** registers 155°F for medium doneness; 165°F for well done (see Cook's Tip). Remove from oven; let stand 5 minutes.

4. Carve pork into thin slices. Arrange tenderloin slices and vegetables on serving platter.

Yield: 8 servings

Nutrients per serving: Calories 240 (29% from fat), Total Fat 8 g, Saturated Fat 2.5 g, Cholesterol 75 mg, Carbohydrate 18 g, Protein 25 g, Sodium 340 mg, Fiber 2 g

Diabetic exchanges per serving: 1 starch, 3 low-fat meat (1 carb)

COOK'S TIPS

The tenderloin is the leanest pork cut available and one of the easiest to prepare. Roasting the meat at a high temperature for a short period of time ensures the meat will remain tender and juicy.

The temperature of the pork will rise approximately 5°F during standing to reach the desired temperatures of 160°F for medium doneness and 170°F for well done. Check the internal temperature of the meat after 25 minutes of roasting to be sure it doesn't become overcooked.

Crushed dried rosemary can be substituted for the Rosemary Herb Seasoning Mix, if desired.

sweet
nothings

You'll be pleased
to share this
assortment of
delightfully tempting
treats as the perfect
ending to any
family meal.

Frozen Peach Melba Pie (p. 108)

COOK'S TIPS

Use the back of a large spoon to help press the crumb mixture firmly onto bottom and up sides of pie plate.

There are so many types of yogurt available that choosing the right one can be confusing. As the name suggests, blended fruit yogurts have the fruit mixed with the yogurt. A low-fat regular or custard-style yogurt can be used for this recipe.

Dipping the peach slices in lemon juice will prevent them from browning.

This dessert can be made and frozen days in advance of serving.

To make cutting this frozen dessert easier, dip the **Utility Knife** into warm water and wipe it dry after cutting each wedge.

Frozen Peach Melba Pie

This delightful frozen dessert captures the flavors of summer in a beautiful way.
(Pictured on p. 106-107)

PREP TIME: 20 MINUTES   BAKE TIME: 12 MINUTES   FREEZE TIME: 6 HOURS

1½ cups finely crushed low-fat honey graham crackers (about forty to forty-five 2⅜ x 1⅛ inch rectangles)

¼ cup peach preserves

1 container (6 ounces) blended fruit raspberry low-fat yogurt

1 container (8 ounces) frozen whipped topping, thawed, divided

1 container (6 ounces) raspberries, divided

2 firm, ripe medium peaches, divided

1 container (6 ounces) blended fruit peach low-fat yogurt

1. Preheat oven to 350°F. Lightly spray **Deep Dish Pie Plate** with nonstick cooking spray. Finely crush graham crackers in large resealable plastic food storage bag using **Baker's Roller®**. Place cracker crumbs in **Small Batter Bowl**; add preserves and mix well. Press crumb mixture evenly and firmly onto bottom and up sides of pie plate. Bake 12 minutes. Cool completely.

2. Place raspberry yogurt in **Classic Batter Bowl**. Fold in 1 cup of the whipped topping; spread evenly over bottom of crust. Reserve 14 raspberries; set aside for garnish. Sprinkle remaining raspberries evenly over raspberry yogurt mixture.

3. Peel one peach and remove pit. Coarsely chop using **Food Chopper**. Place peach yogurt in clean Classic Batter Bowl. Fold in chopped peach and 1 cup of the whipped topping; spread evenly over raspberries. Freeze until firm, about 6 hours or overnight.

4. When ready to serve, let pie stand at room temperature 20 minutes. Cut remaining peach into 16 thin slices; arrange over top of pie in a slightly overlapping circular pattern, leaving center open. Attach open star tip to **Easy Accent® Decorator**; fill with remaining whipped topping. Garnish center and edge of pie with whipped topping. Garnish with reserved raspberries. Cut into wedges.

Yield: 8 servings

Nutrients per serving: Calories 210 (25% from fat), Total Fat 6 g
Saturated Fat 5 g, Cholesterol 5 mg, Carbohydrate 36 g,
Protein 2 g, Sodium 70 mg, Fiber 2 g

Diabetic exchanges per serving: ½ starch, 2 fruit, 1 fat
(2½ carb)

Mint Chocolate Meringues

These little treats simply melt in your mouth, are low in calories and are fat-free. Who can ask for anything more? (Pictured on p. 110)

PREP TIME: 20 MINUTES   BAKE TIME: 1 HOUR   COOL TIME: 30-60 MINUTES

2 large egg whites, room temperature

¼ teaspoon cream of tartar

½ cup sugar

2 tablespoons unsweetened cocoa powder

⅛ teaspoon peppermint or mint extract

1. Preheat oven to 275°F. In **Classic Batter Bowl**, beat egg whites on high speed of electric mixer until very foamy, about 20 seconds. Add cream of tartar and continue to beat 1-2 minutes or until soft peaks form. (Tips of peaks will curl down when beaters are lifted.) Continue beating on high speed, gradually adding sugar in a slow, steady stream. (Do not add all of the sugar at once.) Continue beating on high speed 3-4 minutes or until sugar is dissolved, mixture is glossy and stiff peaks form. (Tips of peaks will remain upright when beaters are lifted.)

2. Place cocoa powder in **Flour/Sugar Shaker**; sprinkle over egg whites. Using **Classic Scraper**, gently fold cocoa powder into egg whites just until cocoa powder disappears. Gently fold in peppermint extract.

3. Cover **Rectangle Stone** with **Parchment Paper**. Attach open star tip to **Easy Accent® Decorator**; fill with meringue mixture. Pipe mixture into small rosettes, about 1½ inches in diameter, 1 inch apart. Refill decorator as needed.

4. Bake 1 hour. Meringues should look dry and have small cracks on the surface. Turn oven off and leave meringues in oven with door slightly ajar for 30-60 minutes or until meringues are thoroughly dry.

Yield: 36 meringue cookies

Nutrients per serving (3 meringues): Calories 35 (2% from fat), Total Fat 0 g, Saturated Fat 0 g, Cholesterol 0 mg, Carbohydrate 8 g, Protein 1 g, Sodium 10 mg, Fiber 0 g

Diabetic exchanges per serving (3 meringues): ½ starch (½ carb)

Variation: *Cinnamon Chocolate Meringues*: Omit peppermint extract. Combine ¼ teaspoon ground cinnamon and sugar in Step 1. Proceed as recipe directs.

COOK'S TIPS

Cream of tartar is a fine white powder that functions as an acid to provide stability and improve the volume of beaten egg whites. It can be found in the spice section of the grocery store.

Eggs will separate more easily when cold; however, they beat to their fullest volume at room temperature. Use the **Egg Separator**, which conveniently attaches to the rim of most bowls, to separate the egg yolk from the egg white. Be careful not to get even a speck of egg yolk into the whites, or they will not beat properly.

For best results, choose a cool, dry day for making meringue cookies. Store meringues in a tightly covered container at room temperature.

Lively Lemon Bars

The bright flavor of lemon seems to personify summer, but you can enjoy this delightful, tea-time dessert any time of the year.

PREP TIME: 15 MINUTES   COOK TIME: 37 MINUTES

Crust

1½	cups all-purpose flour
½	cup powdered sugar
½	cup (1 stick) 70% vegetable oil spread (see Cook's Tip)

Filling

3	lemons
1	cup granulated sugar
2	eggs
2	egg whites
2	tablespoons all-purpose flour
¼	teaspoon salt
2	teaspoons powdered sugar

1. Preheat oven to 350°F. Spray **Square Baker** with nonstick cooking spray. For crust, combine flour and powdered sugar in **Classic Batter Bowl**. Add vegetable oil spread; blend using **Pastry Blender** until mixture resembles coarse crumbs. Press crumb mixture onto bottom of baker. Bake 17 minutes; remove from oven to **Stackable Cooling Rack**.

2. Meanwhile, for filling, zest two of the lemons using **Lemon Zester/Scorer** to measure 2 teaspoons zest. Finely snip zest using **Kitchen Shears**. Juice lemons using **Juicer** to measure ½ cup juice. In **Small Batter Bowl**, combine lemon zest, juice and granulated sugar; whisk using **Stainless Steel Whisk**. Add eggs, egg whites, flour and salt to batter bowl; whisk until blended.

3. Pour filling over crust, spreading evenly. Bake 20 minutes or until filling is set. Remove from oven to cooling rack. Cool completely. Sprinkle with powdered sugar. Cut into bars.

Yield: 16 bars

Nutrients per serving (1 bar): Calories 170 (30% from fat), Total Fat 6 g, Saturated Fat 1 g, Cholesterol 25 mg, Carbohydrate 27 g, Protein 3 g, Sodium 105 mg, Fiber 0 g

Diabetic exchanges per serving (1 bar): 1 starch, 1 fruit, 1 fat (2 carb)

COOK'S TIPS

To reduce calories and fat, this recipe calls for reduced-fat vegetable oil spread that comes in a stick form instead of butter or margarine. We recommend a vegetable oil spread with at least 70% fat. Other products contain too much water, which causes baked goods to become tough.

Store lemon bars in a tightly covered container at room temperature.

Be sure the lemon bars are completely cool before cutting. The **Mini-Serving Spatula** is just the right size for removing the cut bars from the pan.

Keep a **Flour/Sugar Shaker** filled with powdered sugar on hand for a quick, easy and fat-free finish to cakes, cookies and bars.

Mint Chocolate Meringues (p. 109), Lively Lemon Bars

Easy Apple Burritos

This apple dessert, flavored with orange zest and cinnamon, will change the way you think about burritos.

PREP TIME: 15 MINUTES   MICROWAVE TIME: 6-8 MINUTES

3 large Granny Smith apples, sliced (about 4 cups)

2 tablespoons sugar

1 teaspoon *Pantry Korintje Cinnamon*

1 teaspoon 70% vegetable oil spread

1 orange

6 (6-inch) flour tortillas

1½ cups fat-free vanilla frozen yogurt

6 tablespoons fat-free caramel ice cream topping

Additional Pantry Korintje Cinnamon

1. Peel, core and slice apples using **Apple Peeler/Corer/Slicer**; cut apple slices into quarters. Place apples, sugar, cinnamon and vegetable oil spread in **Large Micro-Cooker®**. Microwave, covered, on HIGH 3-4 minutes or until apples are crisp-tender.

2. Zest orange using **Lemon Zester/Scorer** to measure ½ teaspoon zest. Add orange zest to apple mixture; mix gently. Spread ⅓ cup apple mixture down center of each tortilla; roll up tightly. Place burritos in **Square Baker**, seam side down.

3. Microwave, uncovered, on HIGH 3-4 minutes or until heated through. To serve, place burrito on dessert plate. Top with one scoop frozen yogurt; drizzle with 1 tablespoon ice cream topping. Sprinkle with cinnamon. Repeat with remaining burritos. Serve immediately.

Yield: 6 servings

Nutrients per serving: Calories 260 (10% calories from fat), Total Fat 3 g, Saturated Fat .5 g, Cholesterol 0 mg, Carbohydrate 56 g, Protein 6 g, Sodium 230 mg, Fiber 3 g

Diabetic exchanges per serving: 2 starch, 1½ fruit (3½ carb)

LOW FAT
LOW CHOLESTEROL

30 minutes or less

COOK'S TIPS

Ground cinnamon can be substituted for the Korintje Cinnamon, if desired.

To bake burritos in a conventional oven, preheat oven to 350°F. Prepare apples as directed in Step 1. Cook apples, sugar, cinnamon and vegetable oil spread in **Professional (10-in.) Sauté Pan** over medium heat 5-6 minutes or until apples are tender; stir in orange zest. Fill tortillas as directed in Step 2. Bake, covered, 15 minutes or until heated through.

To make an orange twist, score orange from top to bottom using Lemon Zester/Scorer and cut orange into thin slices. Make one cut into each slice, just to the center. Twist slices and use to garnish each dessert.

COOK'S TIPS

For a special touch, add
1/8 teaspoon **Pantry Korintje
Cinnamon** to the granulated
sugar; mix well. Sprinkle
evenly over buttered wonton
squares before baking.

For an elegant presentation,
drizzle fat-free strawberry ice
cream topping over dessert
plates and place two wonton
cups onto each drizzled plate.

Unfilled wonton cups can be
prepared up to 1 week in
advance. Prepare cups as
directed in Step 1. Store
wontons in a resealable
plastic food storage bag or
airtight container at room
temperature. Prepare filling
and fill wonton cups just
before serving.

You can use a variety of
flavored yogurts and fresh
fruit combinations for this
recipe—use your imagination!

Berries 'N Cream Wonton Cups

These dainty desserts will be sensational at bridal showers or dinner parties.

PREP TIME: 15 MINUTES   BAKE TIME: 6-8 MINUTES

24 square wonton wrappers
 1 tablespoon butter or margarine,
    melted
 2 tablespoons granulated sugar
 1 container (8 ounces) low-fat
    strawberry yogurt
1½ cups thawed, frozen whipped
    topping, divided
 1 cup raspberries
½ cup blueberries
 2 teaspoons powdered sugar

1. Preheat oven to 350°F. Using **Pastry
   Brush**, brush one side of each wonton
   wrapper with melted butter. Sprinkle
   wontons evenly with sugar using
   Flour/Sugar Shaker. Press each wonton,
   sugared side up, into cups of **Deluxe
   Mini-Muffin Pan**. Bake 6-8 minutes or
   until edges are light golden brown.
   Remove wontons from pan to **Stackable
   Cooling Rack**; cool completely.

2. Place yogurt in **Small Batter Bowl**; fold
   in 1 cup of the whipped topping. Attach
   closed star tip to **Easy Accent®
   Decorator**; fill with remaining
   whipped topping.

3. Using **Small Scoop**, scoop yogurt
   mixture into each wonton. Top each
   wonton with one raspberry and two
   blueberries. Garnish with whipped
   topping; sprinkle with powdered sugar.
   Serve immediately.

Yield: 24 wontons

Nutrients per serving (2 wonton cups): Calories 110
(24% from fat), Total Fat 3 g, Saturated Fat 2 g,
Cholesterol 5 mg, Carbohydrate 18 g, Protein 2 g,
Sodium 110 mg, Fiber 1 g

Diabetic exchanges per serving (2 wonton cups): 1 starch,
½ fat (1 carb)

Fudgy Glazed Brownies

*Pure indulgence with a fraction of the fat—these brownies are
a dream come true for those watching their waistlines.*

PREP TIME: 15 MINUTES   BAKE TIME: 25-28 MINUTES   COOL TIME: 1 HOUR

Brownies

- 1½ cups all-purpose flour
- 1 cup unsweetened cocoa powder
- ½ teaspoon salt
- 2 eggs
- 4 egg whites
- 3 cups granulated sugar
- ⅔ cup 70% vegetable oil spread, melted
- 1 container (6 ounces) low-fat vanilla yogurt

Glaze

- 1⅓ cups powdered sugar
- ¼ cup unsweetened cocoa powder
- ½ teaspoon vanilla
- 2-3 tablespoons hot water

  Powdered sugar (optional)

1. For brownies, preheat oven to 350°F. Spray bottom of **Stoneware Bar Pan** with nonstick cooking spray. In **Small Batter Bowl**, combine flour, cocoa powder and salt; mix well.

2. In **Classic Batter Bowl**, whisk eggs and egg whites until blended using **Stainless Steel Whisk**. Add sugar, vegetable oil spread and yogurt; whisk until blended. Add flour mixture; mix until well blended.

3. Pour batter into bar pan. Bake 25-28 minutes or until center is set. Do not overbake. Remove from oven to **Stackable Cooling Rack**; cool completely.

4. For glaze, combine powdered sugar, cocoa powder, vanilla and hot water; mix until smooth and spreadable. Spread evenly over surface of cooled brownie using **Small Spreader**. Let stand until frosting is set. Cut into bars.

Yield: 32 bars

Nutrients per serving (1 bar): Calories 160 (22% from fat),
Total Fat 4 g, Saturated Fat 1 g, Cholesterol 15 mg,
Carbohydrate 31 g, Protein 2 g, Sodium 90 mg, Fiber 1 g

Diabetic exchanges per serving (1 bar): 1 starch, 1 fruit, ½ fat
(2 carb)

COOK'S TIPS

For tips on using reduced-fat vegetable oil spread, refer to the Cook's Tip on page 111.

For a finishing touch, create a heart on brownies using our **Cupcake Stencil**. Gently place stencil over glazed brownie squares. Sprinkle with powdered sugar; carefully lift stencil to reveal heart shape.

For even fewer calories, you can omit the frosting and sprinkle brownies with powdered sugar using the **Flour/Sugar Shaker**, if you'd like.

To easily cut brownies, dip the **Utility Knife** into hot water between cuts and wipe dry with a damp paper towel.

This recipe can be easily divided in half and prepared in the **Square Baker**. Divide all ingredients in half, using ⅓ cup yogurt. Prepare brownies as recipe directs. Bake 25-28 minutes or until center is set. To prepare the glaze, simply divide the ingredients in half and prepare as recipe directs.

Angel Food Shortcakes

Angel food cake layers are topped with a fresh strawberry topping that sparkles with a hint of balsamic vinegar.

PREP TIME: 20 MINUTES   BAKE TIME: 30-33 MINUTES   COOL TIME: 2 HOURS

COOK'S TIPS

This cake is best when prepared and served the same day.

Look for plump, ripe but firm strawberries with bright green tops. Refrigerate them in their original container after purchasing.

Gently wash the berries before hulling with the **Cook's Corer®** so they don't become waterlogged. Spread the berries over a paper towel, pat dry and remove hulls. Place each strawberry stem side down in the **Egg Slicer Plus®** and slice.

Strawberry preserves or jelly can be substituted for the sugar-free strawberry preserves, if desired.

For a pretty garnish, fill the **Easy Accent® Decorator** with whipped topping and pipe a rosette onto each serving.

Cake

- 1 orange
- 1 package (16 ounces) angel food cake mix
- 2 tablespoons all-purpose flour
- 1½ cups water
- 1 cup sliced almonds
- 1½ teaspoons powdered sugar (optional)

Topping

- 1 container (1 pound) strawberries, hulled and sliced
- ¼ cup sugar-free strawberry preserves
- 1 tablespoon balsamic vinegar

  Thawed, frozen whipped topping (optional)

  Orange slices and additional orange zest (optional)

1. For cake, preheat oven to 350°F. Line **Stoneware Bar Pan** with a 13-inch piece of **Parchment Paper**. Using **Lemon Zester/Scorer**, zest orange to measure 1 tablespoon zest. In large bowl, combine cake mix, flour, water and zest. Beat at low speed of electric mixer until moistened. Increase speed to medium; beat 1 minute. Pour batter into pan, spreading evenly. Sprinkle almonds evenly over batter. Bake 30-33 minutes or until top springs back when lightly touched with fingertip. Remove from oven to **Stackable Cooling Rack**. Cool 10 minutes. Using edges of paper, carefully lift cake from pan onto cooling rack; cool completely.

2. Place an additional 18-inch piece of Parchment Paper over cake. Place cooling rack over cake and carefully invert cake. Peel Parchment Paper from bottom side of cake; discard. Place **Large Grooved Cutting Board** over cake and invert again so cake is topside up; discard Parchment Paper. Sprinkle powdered sugar over cake using **Flour/Sugar Shaker**, if desired. Cut cake into 2½-inch squares using **Serrated Bread Knife**.

3. For filling, in **Small Batter Bowl**, combine strawberries, preserves and vinegar; mix gently. Let stand 15 minutes.

4. For each serving, place one cake square on dessert plate; top with ¼ cup strawberry mixture. Top with second cake square. Garnish with whipped topping, orange slices and additional orange zest, if desired.

Yield: 12 servings

Nutrients per serving: Calories 210 (20% from fat), Total Fat 5 g, Saturated Fat 0 g, Cholesterol 0 mg, Carbohydrate 39 g, Protein 5 g, Sodium 340 mg, Fiber 2 g

Diabetic exchanges per serving: 1½ starch, 1 fruit, ½ fat (2 carb)

Creamy Cappuccino Cheesecake

With a chocolate cookie crust, coffee-flavored filling and a stenciled cocoa swirl, this cheesecake is as stunning as it is delicious.

PREP TIME: 25 MINUTES BAKE TIME: 1 HOUR, 30 MINUTES
COOL TIME: 2 HOURS CHILL TIME: 6 HOURS

8 reduced-fat creme-filled chocolate sandwich cookies, finely chopped (about ¾ cup)

1½ cups sugar

3 tablespoons all-purpose flour

½ teaspoon *Pantry Korintje Cinnamon*

¼ teaspoon salt

3 packages (8 ounces each) fat-free cream cheese

2 packages (8 ounces) reduced-fat cream cheese (Neufchâtel)

1 cup fat-free sour cream

2 teaspoons vanilla

4 large eggs

½ cup double-strength coffee, cooled

1½ teaspoons unsweetened cocoa powder (optional)

Preheat oven to 325°F. Lightly spray **Springform Pan** with nonstick cooking spray. Place cookies in resealable plastic food storage bag; crush into fine crumbs using **Baker's Roller®**. Press crumbs into bottom of pan. Bake 10 minutes. Remove from oven to **Stackable Cooling Rack**.

2. Meanwhile, in **Small Batter Bowl**, combine sugar, flour, cinnamon and salt. In **Classic Batter Bowl**, beat cream cheese at high speed of electric mixer until smooth. Add sugar mixture to cream cheese; beat well. Add sour cream and vanilla; beat until blended. Add eggs, one at a time; mix at low speed just until blended. Gradually add coffee while mixing at low speed; mix until well blended. Pour filling over crust.

3. Bake 1 hour, 15 minutes–1 hour, 20 minutes or until center appears nearly set when gently shaken (the center will firm as it cools). Remove from oven to cooling rack. Immediately run releasing tool around sides of cake to loosen from pan; cool completely. Loosely cover; refrigerate at least 6 hours or overnight. Release collar from pan.

4. If desired, place **Swirl Stencil** over top of cake. Sprinkle with cocoa powder using **Flour/Sugar Shaker**; carefully remove stencil. Cut into wedges.

Yield: 16 servings

Nutrients per serving: Calories 250 (30% from fat), Total Fat 8 g, Saturated Fat 4.5 g, Cholesterol 80 mg, Carbohydrate 30 g, Protein 12 g, Sodium 430 mg, Fiber 0 g

Diabetic exchanges per serving: 2 starch, 1 medium-fat meat (2 carb)

COOK'S TIPS

If desired, 2 tablespoons instant coffee granules mixed with ½ cup hot water can be substituted for double-strength coffee. Cool completely.

Ground cinnamon can be substituted for Korintje Cinnamon, if desired.

To prevent overbaking, always check cheesecakes at the minimum baking time. When done, the center area will still jiggle slightly. The center will firm as the cheesecake cools.

Gently blot surface of cheesecake with paper towel to remove any extra moisture that may have formed on the surface during refrigeration.

Running the releasing tool immediately after taking the cheesecake out of the oven helps prevent the cheesecake from cracking.

For a smooth cut, dip the **Utility Knife** into warm water and wipe it dry after each cut.

Apple-Cherry Crisp

This cheery dessert is made with ingredients that you may already have on hand.

PREP TIME: 20 MINUTES   BAKE TIME: 35-40 MINUTES

COOK'S TIPS

You'll need about 3 pounds of apples to make this recipe.

Ground cinnamon can be substituted for the Korintje Cinnamon, if desired.

Fruit Filling

- 6 medium Granny Smith apples, sliced (about 8 cups)
- 1 can (21 ounces) cherry pie filling
- ½ teaspoon *Pantry Korintje Cinnamon*

Streusel Topping

- ¼ cup (½ stick) 70% vegetable oil spread, melted
- ¼ cup sliced almonds, chopped
- 1 cup old-fashioned or quick oats
- ¼ cup all-purpose flour
- ¼ cup packed brown sugar
- ½ teaspoon Pantry Korintje Cinnamon
- Fat-free vanilla frozen yogurt (optional)

1. Preheat oven to 375°F. For fruit filling, peel, core and slice apples using **Apple Peeler/Corer/Slicer**. Cut apples in half. Combine apples, pie filling and cinnamon in large **Colander Bowl**; mix gently. Spoon filling into **Deep Dish Baker**.

2. For streusel topping, place vegetable oil spread in **Small Micro-Cooker**®. Microwave on HIGH 45-60 seconds or until melted. Chop almonds using **Food Chopper**. Add almonds, oats, flour, brown sugar and cinnamon to micro-cooker; mix well. Sprinkle topping evenly over fruit filling.

3. Bake 35-40 minutes or until apples are tender. Cool slightly. Serve warm topped with frozen yogurt, if desired.

Yield: 8 servings

Nutrients per serving: Calories 280 (24% from fat), Total Fat 8 g, Saturated Fat 1.5 g, Cholesterol 0 mg, Carbohydrate 51 g, Protein 3 g, Sodium 70 mg, Fiber 4 g

Diabetic exchanges per serving: 1 starch, 2½ fruit, 1 fat (3½ carb)

COOK'S TIPS

Use the **Egg Separator** to easily separate the egg whites from the yolks, which contain fat and cholesterol.

Lemons kept at room temperature will yield more juice than those that are refrigerated.

To help release the juice from a lemon, using even pressure, roll the lemon between the palm of your hand and the **Cutting Board**. Cut the lemon in half crosswise and juice it using the Juicer.

Lemon Blueberry Pudding Cake

This moist, homestyle dessert has a twist of fresh flavor with berries and lemon.

PREP TIME: 10 MINUTES   BAKE TIME: 35-40 MINUTES

Cake & Filling

- 1 can (21 ounces) blueberry pie filling
- 1 package (18.25 ounces) lemon cake mix
- 3 egg whites
- 1 cup water
- 1/3 cup vegetable oil

Pudding

- 1 lemon
- 1 cup boiling water
- 1 package (3 ounces) lemon gelatin
- 2 teaspoons powdered sugar
  Thawed, fat-free frozen whipped topping (optional)

1. Preheat oven to 375°F. Lightly spray **Rectangular Baker** with nonstick cook spray. For cake and filling, spread pie filling over bottom of baker. In **Classic Batter Bowl**, combine cake mix, egg whites, water and oil; whisk until smooth using **Stainless Steel Whisk**. Pour batter evenly over pie filling.

2. For pudding, zest lemon using **Lemon Zester/Scorer** to measure 1 tablespoon zest. Juice lemon using **Juicer** to measure 2 tablespoons juice. In **Small Micro-Cooker®**, microwave water on HIGH 1-2 minutes or until boiling. Add gelatin; mix until completely dissolved. Add lemon zest and juice to gelatin mixture; pour evenly over top of batter.

3. Bake 35-40 minutes or until **Cake Tester** inserted in center of cake comes out clean. Remove from oven; let stand 10 minutes. Lightly sprinkle with powdered sugar using **Flour/Sugar Shaker**. Serve warm with whipped topping, if desired.

Yield: 15 servings

Nutrients per serving: Calories 250 (28% from fat), Total Fat 8 g, Saturated Fat 1.5 g, Cholesterol 0 mg, Carbohydrate 42 g, Protein 3 g, Sodium 250 mg, Fiber 1 g

Diabetic exchanges per serving: 1 starch, 2 fruit, 1 fat (3 car

Recipe Index

About Our Recipes

The preparation and cooking times at the beginning of each recipe serve as a helpful guide when planning your time in the kitchen. Many of our recipes can be prepared in 30 minutes or less and are accompanied by a symbol indicating this. As an important first step, we suggest you read through the recipe and assemble the necessary ingredients and equipment. "Prep time" is the approximate amount of time needed to prepare recipe ingredients before the "Cook time." Prep time includes active steps such as chopping and mixing. It can also include cooking ingredients for a recipe that is assembled and then baked. Some preparation steps can be done simultaneously or during cooking and are usually indicated by the word "meanwhile." Some recipes that have steps not easily separated have a combined "Prep and cook time."

Notes on Nutrition

The nutrition information in *It's Good for You* can help you decide how specific recipes can fit into your overall meal plan. The nutrient values for each recipe were derived from The Food Processor, Version 8.1 (ESHA Research), or are provided by food manufacturers. In addition to listing calories, total fat, saturated fat, cholesterol, carbohydrate, protein, sodium and fiber, we include diabetic exchanges commonly used by people with diabetes. This information is based on the most current dietary guidelines, *Exchange Lists for Meal Planning (1995)*, by the American Diabetes Association and the American Dietetic Association. For each recipe, two lists of exchanges are provided. The first option is based on the traditional method of figuring diabetic exchanges; the second option is given in parentheses and reflects the newer system of carbohydrate counting. When using either approach to meal planning, always consult with your physician, registered dietitian, or certified diabetes educator who will address your individual needs.

Nutritional analysis for each recipe is based on the first ingredient listed whenever a choice is given and does not include optional ingredients, ingredients followed by the words "to taste," garnishes, fat used to grease pans, or serving suggestions.

Metric Conversion Chart

Volume Measurements (dry)	Volume Measurements (fluid)	Dimensions
⅛ teaspoon = 0.6 mL	1 fluid ounce (2 tablespoons) = 30 mL	⅛ inch = 3 mm
¼ teaspoon = 1.25 mL	4 fluid ounces (½ cup) = 125 mL	¼ inch = 6 mm
½ teaspoon = 2.5 mL	8 fluid ounces (1 cup) = 250 mL	½ inch = 1 cm
¾ teaspoon = 3.75 mL	12 fluid ounces (1½ cups) = 375 mL	¾ inch = 2 cm
1 teaspoon = 5 mL	16 fluid ounces (2 cups) = 500 mL	1 inch = 2.5 cm
1 tablespoon = 15 mL		**Oven Temperatures**
2 tablespoons = 30 mL	**Weights (mass)**	250°F = 120°C
¼ cup = 50 mL	1 ounce = 30 g	275°F = 140°C
⅓ cup = 75 mL	4 ounces = 125 g	300°F = 150°C
½ cup = 125 mL	8 ounces = 250 g	325°F = 160°C
⅔ cup = 150 mL	12 ounces = 350 g	350°F = 180°C
¾ cup = 175 mL	16 ounces = 1 pound = 500 g	375°F = 190°C
1 cup = 250 mL		400°F = 200°C
		425°F = 220°C
		450°F = 230°C

Recipes in this cookbook have not been tested using metric measures. When converting and preparing recipes with metric measures, some variations in quality may be noticed.